M000012522

AFTER NET NEUTRALITY

AFTER NET NEUTRALITY

A NEW DEAL FOR

THE DIGITAL AGE

VICTOR PICKARD AND

DAVID ELLIOT BERMAN

Yale UNIVERSITY PRESS   NEW HAVEN AND LONDON

Published with assistance from the foundation established in memory of
Amasa Stone Mather of the Class of 1907, Yale College.

Yale University Press books may be purchased in quantity for educational,
business, or promotional use. For information, please e-mail sales.press@
yale.edu (U.S. office) or sales@yaleup.co.uk (U.K. office).

Designed by Nancy Ovedovitz and set in Scala and The Sans types by
Integrated Publishing Solutions. Printed in the United States of America.

Library of Congress Control Number: 2019936695

ISBN 978-0-300-24140-2 (hardcover : alk. paper)

A catalogue record for this book is available from the British Library.
This paper meets the requirements of ANSI/NISO Z39.48-1992
(Permanence of Paper).

10 9 8 7 6 5 4 3 2 1

CONTENTS

INTRODUCTION

In the summer of 2018, a dystopian illustration of what our post–net neutrality future might look like materialized in Santa Clara County, California. That July, a wildfire broke out in the region. The Santa Clara Fire Department was dispatched to fight the blaze and used its Verizon cell phone network to help coordinate the deployment of trucks, emergency personnel, and other critical resources from all over the state. Firefighters quickly noticed that their internet access had slowed significantly. Though they had paid for an unlimited data plan, Verizon reduced the fire department's internet speed to less than 1/200 of normal download rates. The fire department contacted Verizon, which confirmed that it was slowing down the connection and informed the department that it would continue to do so unless it switched to a new data plan at more than twice the price.[1]

We should anticipate more of this brazen abuse of power in the future. A small handful of private corporations owns the pipelines over which speech, commerce, and expression on the internet flow. In the wake of the Federal Communications Commission's (FCC) 2017 decision to repeal net neutrality, these companies have been given carte blanche to censor internet traffic as they see fit. It is reasonable to assume that they will do just that—unless we, as a democratic society, stop them.

Enter Net Neutrality

Few policy battles have captured the public's imagination like net neutrality.[2] From comedian John Oliver's thirteen-minute viral rant on net neutrality to internet memes skewering Federal Communications Commission chairman Ajit Pai, the debate over who owns and controls the pipes that connect Americans to the internet has seeped into mainstream culture unlike any controversy in the history of telecommunications. Nonetheless, many observers still view net neutrality as a wonky technical debate instead of one over fundamental democratic principles and freedoms. In fact, the debate over net neutrality speaks directly to a core social contract between the government, internet service providers (ISPs), and the public. Our book aims to clarify why net neutrality matters and what is to be done about it.

But first, a general definition: net neutrality refers to the basic principle that ISPs should not unreasonably discriminate against legal internet traffic and online communication, regardless of its source or destination. In many ways, net neutrality is embodied in the technical design of the internet itself. The internet was built according to the simple but brilliant "end-to-end" principle, which holds that the "intelligence" of a network exists on its edges—in the users and applications that send traffic over the network.[3] The "core" of the network acts as "dumb pipes," as passive infrastructure that merely funnels traffic to the edges of the network. In short, the internet was engineered to maximize the liberty of users while limiting the power of network owners and operators to manipulate traffic.

As a policy principle, net neutrality serves as an essential safeguard that prevents ISPs from interfering with the traffic that flows through their wires. Net neutrality gives the FCC the regulatory authority to prevent the likes of Comcast and Verizon from slowing down ("throttling") or blocking users' access to content. Net neutrality also prevents ISPs from pressuring websites to pay for faster streaming and load times, an extortion scheme that is euphemistically called "paid prioritization."

This practice creates fast lanes for wealthier companies that can afford to pay up, leaving everyone else stuck in the internet's slow lane.

Slow lanes are far more than a nuisance for internet users: they have the potential to dramatically alter our political, social, and civic lives. Numerous studies show that the longer it takes for a website to load, the more likely it is that visitors will simply navigate elsewhere. A delay of just a few seconds can cause a website to lose upwards of one-third of its traffic.[4] Allowing ISPs to divide the internet into fast and slow lanes will inevitably amplify the voices, ideas, and worldviews of those with power and resources, while marginalizing those without them.

Thus, while some view net neutrality merely as a technical debate over how we should manage the thousands of miles of wire that power the internet in the United States, we argue that net neutrality bears directly on some of the most fundamental normative and political questions that every democratic society must answer. Who has the power to speak in the public sphere? How can we ensure widespread access to the information that is needed to sustain a self-governing populace? Can the communications infrastructure that is needed to support a democratic society be entrusted to self-interested corporations? If not, what alternatives are there?

Although net neutrality is itself not sufficient for dealing with the manifold threats to internet freedom posed by monopolistic

ISPs (to say nothing of platform monopolies such as Google and Facebook), it is nonetheless, in our view, a crucial prerequisite. As we will discuss, a world without net neutrality is one that imperils the internet's democratic potential. Losing net neutrality subjects the most important information and communication infrastructure of the twenty-first century to the profit-seeking whims of a small number of large commercial firms.

The unfolding of the net neutrality saga since the early 2000s—its many twists and turns, dramatic moments, and activist hijinks—is a fascinating case study. But it is also, at times, downright confusing. Between the technical jargon, reams of industry talking points, legalistic-sounding distinctions between Title I "information services" and Title II "telecommunications services," and the thick web of political obfuscation that has engulfed much of the battle over net neutrality, the entire story could benefit from some clarification. This book aims to do just that: explain how we got here and what we need to do to push forward.

Overview of the Book

This book provides a concise and comprehensive overview of the history, politics, and ongoing activism around net neutrality.[5] It is impossible to cover every technical and political detail from the nearly two-decade net neutrality debate—a debate that is still, even as we write, a moving target—in the U.S. and beyond.

A complete account requires a much longer book, or perhaps a series of books, but we try to cover the most salient aspects, with an emphasis on the policy roots, economic structures, and social forces driving the debate. This book is, admittedly, an American-centric account of net neutrality. While we focus on net neutrality in the context of the United States, our analysis holds implications for net neutrality battles in other countries as well. We also note at various points how the current trajectory in the United States reflects a degree of "American exceptionalism" when compared to other leading democracies.

Our objective is not just to describe the net neutrality debate; we also aim to change it. While some scholarship on net neutrality draws on theories of law and economics that prioritize considerations of market efficiency, economic growth, competition, and innovation, our analysis favors principles of equality, distributive justice, civil rights, and democratic participation.[6] Too often the existing literature frames net neutrality, at least implicitly, as a drama between "good" innovators and content creators such as Google, Facebook, and Netflix, which use and want to protect the internet's open architecture, and "bad" internet service providers such as Comcast and Verizon.[7] This "clash of the titans" narrative foregrounds the actions and economic interests of large corporations while writing out the role of grassroots activists. While much of our emphasis is on the push and pull between the FCC and telecommunication monopolies, which may at times seem like a struggle between elites, we also try to examine this history from the bottom up, drawing attention to the social movements, activists, and concerned citizens who have propelled the net neutrality debate forward.

We turn to the long history of U.S. communication policy to resituate the rollback of net neutrality as part of the broader transformation of American political and economic life over the last several decades as well as indicative of a longer historical trajectory that pits corporate power against government oversight and the public interest. In so doing, we show that the fight against net neutrality is much more than a conflict between the likes of Google and Comcast: it is part of the much wider project to commercialize the public sphere and undermine the possibility of a democratic communication system.

ONE
THE BATTLE FOR OWNERSHIP AND CONTROL OF COMMUNICATION INFRASTRUCTURES

Given the remarkable capabilities of digital media, some analysts believe that the policy problems posed by the internet are entirely novel. However, in many ways, the net neutrality debate is merely the latest iteration in a series of historical confrontations between the corporate owners of communication infrastructures, government regulators, and the public. It is also a clash between two different ideological positions, which might be called "social democratic" and "corporate libertarian" approaches to media policy.[1]

Corporate libertarianism assumes that corporations possess individual freedoms, such as First Amendment free speech rights, that protect them from government oversight and regulation. Proponents of corporate libertarianism see monopolistic corporations not only as deserving winners in a free market economy but also as the main drivers of economic growth and the apotheosis of American freedom. Although corporate libertarianism has a long history, it crystallized during a critical moment in the 1940s when a handful of corporations captured the "new media" of that day: radio broadcasting. Implicit in the corporate libertarian policy paradigm is that government should never intervene in markets—especially in media markets. However, the government is *always* involved: the real questions are *how* it should be involved and in whose interests should it act? In other words, our communication systems are always regulated. In fact, corporate libertarians are actually quite comfortable with state intervention—as long as government limits itself to enhancing the profits of communication oligopolies. This logic maps on neatly to neoliberalism, a reactionary political project that has been ascendant for the past fifty years, which encourages the privatization of public services, a retreat of the regulatory state, and the commercialization of all facets of our daily lives.

Accordingly, just as the government handed over control of radio broadcasting to a corporate oligopoly in the 1930s and 1940s, the internet's infrastructure was largely privatized in the 1990s. This privatization of what had been largely a public resource speaks to a core contradiction of the corporate libertarian position. While the predominant origin myth of the internet tends to portray its birth as the stuff of tinkerers in garages and bold entrepreneurs, in actuality the internet is largely the creation of massive public subsidies. It could have been no other way: government has the luxury of taking on long-term scientific and technological projects that the private sector is loath to pursue due to its focus on generating short-term profits.[2]

The U.S. government initially subsidized the internet's early development through military expenditures. The Advanced Research Projects Agency (ARPA; it later changed its name to the Defense Advanced Research Projects Agency, DARPA) created ARPANET, which invented the basic protocols for today's internet. This system used nonproprietary, open technologies based on principles of interconnection and nondiscrimination. Because there was no profit motive driving its development, there was little incentive to close off the networks. As the network grew, it became more useful and more researchers at universities across the country wanted to join it. The U.S. government continued to subsidize the internet's build-out directly via the National Science Foundation, spending $160 million to create NSFNET, which became the internet's backbone. Public subsidies from other sources such as state governments and state-funded universities likely approached $2 billion.[3] In the early 1990s, this publicly subsidized communication infrastructure was handed over to a few major corporations. Although the

internet was not originally built for commercial purposes,
the rapid privatization of the NSFNET backbone transformed
the underlying logic of the internet to something that primarily served the profit-seeking imperatives of corporate
firms.[4]

In contrast to corporate libertarianism, a social democratic
policy paradigm assumes that some public services are too vital
to leave up to the profit-driven—and oftentimes discriminatory—
logics of the market. It sees an active and progressive role for
government in organizing economic life, finding its greatest
expression in the United States during President Franklin
Delano Roosevelt's New Deal in the 1930s and 1940s. Government policies at this time typically sought to redistribute wealth
and economic power to promote greater egalitarianism. Driven
by a diverse array of social movements, policymakers at that time
attempted to regulate and de-commercialize various aspects of
the American media system.

A social democratic logic treats information as a public good.
In a strictly economic sense, this means that information is
often nonexcludable (it is difficult to exclude free riders from
accessing information), and it is nonrivalrous (one person's
consumption of information does not detract from another's).
A healthy democratic society requires diverse sources of news
so that we can make informed decisions about everything from

whom we vote for to how we conduct our daily lives. It also
depends on citizens having access to reliable information, which
is often expensive to produce, and requires significant physical
capital—printing presses, broadcasting equipment, and so forth—
as well as human capital, including news reporters, editors, and
camera operators. Left to its own devices, the private sector is
likely to produce the amount of information that the market
dictates, not the amount that democracy requires (for example,
where all members of a polity have equal access to multiple
news outlets offering diverse points of views on pressing social
matters—a far cry from what Americans have today). This under-
production of information is a form of "market failure" that,
even according to neoclassical economic theory, justifies government intervention.

Given the drawbacks of a purely commercial system, democratic societies should not allow the production and dissemina-
tion of information to be left entirely to the vicissitudes of the
market, especially when a handful of large corporations dominate it and competition is weak or nonexistent. Government is
supposed to protect public goods, guaranteeing their provision
and placing safeguards that prevent commercial logics from cor-
rupting them. However, throughout history, social democratic
and corporate libertarian policy paradigms have come into sharp
conflict over how to regulate telecommunication and media

systems such as the telegraph, telephone, and broadcasting. These clashing positions help set the backdrop for how the net neutrality debate has unfolded in the United States.

A Long History of Net Neutrality

To understand net neutrality—a phrase that was coined in 2002 by Tim Wu to describe what were, in fact, very old principles—it is necessary to situate it within a much longer history.[5] Nondiscrimination principles for communication infrastructures trace back to the age-old legal doctrine of "common carriage," which emerged from medieval British common law. Although initially common carrier laws were applied to transportation networks such as railroads and ports, many nations later applied them to telecommunication networks. This approach generally stemmed from the belief that essential services should be offered to everyone on the same terms. However, the temptation of network operators to abuse their position as gatekeeper—by setting up discriminatory practices that allow them to profit from privileging some types of content and groups of people over others—is also an ancient concern.

Indeed, the efforts of telecommunication providers to achieve market dominance at great social costs have a long history. Often they have come into conflict with government's attempts to impose public interest protections, and public pressure from below seeking to establish a more reliable, affordable, and democratic

system. The arrangements resulting from these ongoing conflicts varied over the years, but the larger power structure often
remained intact. Monopolistic network owners sought to maximize profits, often by denying equal access to their services.

Courts, legislators, and regulatory agencies have interpreted
common carriage in different ways since the dawn of telecommunications. Competing regulatory models at play throughout
this history included regulated monopoly, public ownership,
government-enforced market competition, and corporate libertarianism (or some version of laissez-faire). The U.S. Post
Office's institutional development—in some ways a response
to popular pressure for equal treatment of rural and urban
households—enshrined principles of nondiscrimation.[6] However, a different logic guided both the telegraph and the telephone's early development, which involved multiple levels of
government responding to episodes of popular anger against
corporate power. In particular, public concerns focused on
unequal access to communication networks that were the result
of both limited network build-out and high rates.[7]

In the first Gilded Age, owners of communication networks
were able to assert their dominance over regional markets by
undercutting or even blocking potential rivals from using their
infrastructure. The conflict came to the fore in the late 1800s
when Western Union's ownership of telegraph trunk lines
across the country gave it nearly total control of the network. In

response to Western Union's tendency to overcharge and under-serve the public, a popular movement for "postal telegraphy"—a government-owned telegraph system—peaked in the 1880s with widespread support from not only telegraph users but also groups such as the Knights of Labor and the Populist Party.[8] To maintain its dominant market position, Western Union bought up competing companies and sought to undercut congressional and popular support for constructing a rival publicly owned telegraph system. In the absence of regulatory constraints, Western Union was able to indulge in a number of discriminatory business practices, such as serving only wealthy business clients.[9]

The rise of telephony in the late nineteenth and early twentieth centuries recapitulated some of the political problems posed by telegraphy. However, due to a combination of government regulation and social pressure from below, the new communication system took a different trajectory. With the Bell system (also referred to as AT&T) becoming the largest telephone operator in the world, federal, state, and municipal governments had to determine what kind of social contract should govern this increasingly vital communication network. Most states established public utility commissions to oversee local telephone services, but these agencies were often co-opted.[10]

More effective pressure came from local communities, labor groups, independent telephone service providers, and individual users who mounted quite visible challenges to Bell's dominance. For example, in the 1880s various groups of telephone users launched relentless strikes against unfair pricing and billing practices. Often led by labor groups, these strikes were essentially consumer boycotts.[11] The late 1800s also witnessed a surge of independent commercial and nonprofit cooperative telephone enterprises, especially in the American West and Midwest.[12]

Into the early 1900s, the Bell-independent rivalry led to a rapid expansion of telephone networks.[13] However, AT&T's Bell system often refused to interconnect with independent operators with which it competed for local phone customers. Although independent phone companies initially offered lower rates, Bell could afford to sacrifice its short-term profits to preserve its long-term control of the market simply by cutting its rates wherever it faced a rival. Nonetheless, there was a fierce battle between the "Bell octopus" and independent operators across the U.S. and Canada.[14]

In addition to the rise of independent telephony, strong movements for municipalizing telephone services at the local level rose up to contest Bell's monopoly power. From roughly the 1890s to the end of World War I, municipal ownership of local telephone networks—sometimes part of a broader agenda advanced by progressive, populist, anti-monopoly, and "municipal home rule" movements—remained on the political agenda in many communities and cities across the U.S.[15]

Another strong movement for a public alternative in the early
1900s aimed to "postalize" or nationalize telephony at the federal level. This movement for public ownership reached its peak
in 1918 when the government briefly nationalized Bell (partly
rationalized as a military necessity), placing it under a branch of
the Post Office. However, the experiment was short-lived (only
lasting about one year), partly due to political shifts that helped
turn public opinion against government ownership. The failure
of postalization ultimately cemented private corporate ownership of the nation's telecommunication networks.[16]

During these same years, Bell's anti-competitive behavior
attracted the attention of the federal government, which was
beginning to scrutinize monopolies, even breaking them up,
as it did in the case of Standard Oil in 1911. In response to the
federal investigation of its growing monopoly power over the
nation's phone services, in 1913 Bell reached an out-of-court
settlement with the government, generally referred to as the
Kingsbury Commitment.[17] To maintain its monopoly status, Bell
(hereafter referred to as AT&T) agreed to divest itself of Western
Union, refrain from purchasing other telephone companies
without the Interstate Commerce Commission's approval, and
allow independent local telephone companies to interconnect
with its long-distance network. Despite popular narratives that
it amounted to a capitulation to AT&T, revisionist historians
observe that this regulatory intervention was actually a signifi-

cant blow to the company.[18] Furthermore, enshrining interconnection as a foundational principle was a major advance. But the
settlement also locked in AT&T's market power and indirectly
helped derail local efforts to assert control over the telephone
market. In addition to preventing the government from breaking up the burgeoning AT&T monopoly, the Kingsbury Commitment blunted the growing call for the government to nationalize
America's telephone networks.

As a regulated monopoly, AT&T maintained dominance in
the telephone market. It did so not simply by providing a better
service than its competitors but by buying up the competition,
evading government regulation, engaging in predatory pricing,
centralizing network control, and dominating a nationally inter-
connected network that allowed it to further benefit from "network effects."[19] These actions allowed AT&T's Bell system to
rapidly increase its market share in the early twentieth century
to become an economic and political powerhouse.[20] Dan Schiller
notes, "In the face of the AT&T juggernaut, regulation seemed a
palpable failure."[21] This massive amount of concentrated corporate power would again incur government scrutiny beginning in
the New Deal era, during which AT&T's market dominance was
both challenged and deepened.

An important development during the New Deal era was
the passage of the Communications Act of 1934, which created
the Federal Communications Commission. The FCC became

the main regulatory agency that oversees major communication systems such as telecommunications and broadcasting. The Communications Act also established basic protections against the abuse of monopoly power as well as defending the ever-elusive ideal of the "public interest." Nonetheless, despite the FCC's New Deal origins, President Franklin D. Roosevelt devoted relatively little attention to it during the commission's early years, and the agency was less aggressive than other New Deal regulatory bodies. Some scholars have pointed out that the FCC did not initially pursue a reformist agenda; rather, it even helped solidify commercial radio interests.[22] The inveterate media reformer Everett Parker, recalling how the FCC's genesis was characterized by close ties to media corporations, quipped that of the then seven-person agency, "four commissioners were vetted by AT&T and three by broadcasters."[23] Nonetheless, the FCC actually did exhibit regulatory independence toward AT&T, as we will see below.

The FCC was tasked with regulating interstate and foreign communications services as well as overseeing the regulatory standards for different categories of those services, which fall under different titles (or sections) of the Communications Act of 1934. Title I and Title II are the sections that are most implicated in the net neutrality debate. Title I of the Communications Act covers general provisions of the FCC's responsibilities. Title II specifically covers common carriers, which are subject to much stricter oversight and regulation, including some degree of non-discrimination. This distinction stipulated: "All charges, practices, classifications, and regulations for and in connection with such communication service, shall be just and reasonable."[24]

The FCC's definition of common carriers brings into focus the roots of net neutrality. Firms that were classified as common carriers were prevented from interfering with or discriminating against the content flowing through their channels. The Communications Act determined that it would be "unlawful for any common carrier to make any unjust or unreasonable discrimination in charges, practices, classifications, regulations, facilities, or services for or in connection with like communication service, directly or indirectly." And this held true for "any means or device." Moreover, it was unlawful for common carriers "to make or give any undue or unreasonable preference or advantage to any particular person, class of persons, or locality, or to subject any particular person, class of persons, or locality to any undue or unreasonable prejudice or disadvantage."[25]

Despite accommodating the commercial radio oligopoly from its inception, the early FCC took a decidedly more proactive stance toward telecommunications. In its 1935 AT&T investigation—referred to as the Walker Report, named after the lead investigator, FCC commissioner Paul Walker—the FCC directly confronted AT&T's market power.[26] After the Senate Interstate Commerce Committee allocated $750,000 for the investigation and President Roosevelt signed it into action, the *New York Times* reported that it was "expected to be the most comprehensive study of communication companies and their relationships to each other and to holding companies that has ever been undertaken."[27] The FCC's mandate was to study a number of potentially harmful business practices, including the rates that AT&T charged its customers. The report damaged AT&T's reputation by drawing public attention to its monopoly power and showing how the company's equipment subsidiary Western Electric Company overcharged subscribers $51 million per year (nearly $1 billion in 2019 dollars).[28] Ultimately, the FCC watered down the Walker Report in its final published version. It did, however, find that AT&T had actively hindered regulatory efforts and that its profits were "unusually high for a system engaged in rendering public service."[29]

As an outgrowth of the earlier FCC investigation, AT&T once again came under investigation in the 1940s, this time by the Department of Justice. The inquiry culminated in the DOJ filing suit against AT&T in 1949. The lawsuit was not resolved until the 1956 consent decree, which allowed the company to maintain its monopoly but forced it to share all of its patents royalty-free, a significant triumph for the public interest. AT&T again came under scrutiny in an antitrust case initiated against the company in 1974 and decided in 1982. This time the outcome

was severely structural—AT&T was forced to break up into "Baby
Bells" in what was the most significant antitrust action in the
history of American telecommunications.

The long historical trajectory of these ongoing struggles casts
into stark relief long-standing—and well-founded—concerns
about communication monopolies abusing their market position
to the detriment of society. Until its 1984 divestiture, AT&T was
permitted to dominate the telecommunications industry in part
because many (especially AT&T itself) considered the company
to be a "natural monopoly." Natural monopolies require significant costs up front to construct the core system, but once that
is built, it is relatively inexpensive to add new customers to the
network. Many consider utilities, such as electricity, natural
monopolies because they require large fixed capital expenditures
to establish plant and equipment facilities, but otherwise face low
marginal costs.[30] Thus according to this theory, it is often socially
optimal for one firm to invest in and maintain these services.

Instead of breaking up natural monopolies, regulatory incen-
tives and penalties can be employed to prevent them from ex-
ploiting their market power and induce them to provide public
services. In such cases, government may grant telecommunications companies a monopoly in exchange for abiding by certain
public interest provisions. With the rise of telephony, government enforced common carriage (not officially codified in law

until 1910) so that telecommunication companies could not discriminate against customers willing to pay for services.[31] Universal-service mandates (a term that AT&T co-opted in the early 1900s as a justification for its domination of American telephony) also forced AT&T to build out its network to far-flung and less profitable communities—a protection that is sorely lacking today, as ISPs systematically underserve less profitable communities outside of affluent areas, a practice called "digital redlining."[32]

Another important antecedent for net neutrality was the FCC's three Computer Inquiries, a series of investigations that began in 1966 and culminated in the late 1980s. These proceedings sought to assess whether the growing importance of computers in communication systems would require a change in the FCC's regulatory role, and established the boundaries and relationships between the regulated telecommunications industry and the unregulated computer services industry.[33] The FCC feared that common carriers such as AT&T could engage in anti-competitive practices by privileging their own data processing activities. The FCC therefore attempted to enact a structural separation between "pure communications" and "pure data processing" services. The problem was that computer processing was increasingly involved in both communication and data transmission.

In 1976, the second of these inquiries put forth rules that foreshadowed the current distinction between "information"

and "telecommunications" services. In this investigation, the
FCC decided to divide communication into two legal categories:
"basic services" and "enhanced services." According to this cate-
gorization, basic services were voice telephone services that
merely carried information. Enhanced services included information and computation that altered or added to the data carried by
the underlying infrastructure, such as voice mail.[34] This layered
model of regulation subjected the data that was transmitted over
the basic telecommunications infrastructure to far less regulation than the infrastructure itself. Ultimately, throughout these
inquiries, the market-liberalizing FCC steadily curtailed its earlier
concern with nondiscrimination by establishing a rapidly growing
zone of activity that fell outside of common carrier protections.
The Computer Inquiries thus laid a foundation for subsequent
efforts to abandon common carrier responsibilities even though
the internet has increasingly taken over many of the telecommunications services that had been regulated under Title II.[35]

Two decades later, another fateful change in nomenclature
reflected the creeping influence of corporate libertarianism over
telecommunications policy. With the deregulatory zeal that
characterized 1980s media policy largely continuing under
subsequent Republican and Democratic administrations alike,
Congress passed the Telecommunications Act of 1996, the first
major overhaul of the landmark 1934 Communications Act.
Purportedly an attempt to reform U.S. media policy for the

digital era, the bill passed Congress with significant bipartisan support and was signed into law by President Bill Clinton. The law renamed the two categories established by the Computer Inquiry proceedings so that basic services became "telecommunications services" (still subject to strict common carrier regulation) and enhanced services became lightly regulated "information services." The 1996 Telecommunications Act deregulated cable rates and removed key broadcast ownership limits, leading to massive consolidation. However, the historical importance of common carriage in curbing market excesses was still widely acknowledged, and even the deregulatory thrust of the 1996 Telecommunications Act left the principle of nondiscrimination intact.[36]

The Battle for Net Neutrality Begins

What these historical episodes show us is that in the absence of strong public interest regulations, communication monopolies—like all monopolies—typically have tried to crush competition and exploit their monopoly power.[37] This history also shows us that popular movements have had some success in challenging the commercial excesses of telecommunication monopolies. The desire of network owners to exploit their control over their infrastructure was prevented to some degree by maintaining common carriage rules. These rules, though predating the internet by decades (or, in the case of transportation networks, by centuries), presage the importance of net neutrality. As common carriers, telephone operators were forbidden from interfering with or discriminating against the content flowing through their channels. Since telephone service is classified as a Title II common carrier, initially internet service that was provided over telephone lines (either through dial-up internet or DSL) was also subject to common carrier laws. This classification empowered the FCC to protect the principle of nondiscrimination by preventing telephone service providers from blocking or throttling traffic.

However, as the internet rapidly expanded and its commercial value increased, the desire of telecommunication companies to exert greater control over their infrastructure also magnified. This was especially true of cable companies, which did not want to be regulated as stringently as telephone service providers. In 2002, the Republican-appointed FCC chairman Michael Powell led the effort to reclassify internet access provided over cable wires as an "information service." As noted above, information services fall under Title I of the Communications Act, which does not include the strict consumer protections of Title II. The FCC's 3-1 party-line vote (the second Democratic commissioner had yet to be appointed) to reclassify cable ISPs as a Title I information service left the FCC with few regulatory tools to protect cable broadband customers. The sudden policy change deeply troubled Commissioner Michael Copps, the lone dissenter. He offered a dire warning about the dangers of failing to regulate America's communications infrastructure: "Today we take a gigantic leap down the road of removing core communications services from the statutory frameworks established by Congress . . . and playing a game of regulatory musical chairs." Copps presciently cautioned that "how America deploys broadband is the central infrastructure challenge our country faces," calling the issue "a public policy matter of enormous implications." These implications included everything from consumer choice to whether disadvantaged groups have the same opportunity to "share fully in our general prosperity."[38]

For the most part, the cable industry—which had long lobbied for and helped bring about this change—celebrated the decision, while public interest advocates roundly condemned it.[39] Reformers such as Copps articulated a critique that went beyond concerns about the loss of consumer protections to underscore the glaring contradictions in anti–net neutrality arguments: "Many in industry and government prescribe closing off Internet openness [as] a cure for telecom's ills. They claim that all they are doing is 'letting the market reign supreme,' and 'deregulating,' deploying the rhetoric of Libertarianism to serve their agenda." Copps noted a central flaw in the libertarian position: "They are fond of railing against picking winners and losers when they are in fact picking winners and losers themselves. . . . I believe that if the Commission's present mind-set is fully implemented, we

will look back, shake our heads and wonder whatever happened
to that open, dynamic and liberating Internet that once we knew.
'What promise it held,' we'll say. If that happens, history won't
forgive us. Nor should it."[40]

Meanwhile, some smaller, independent cable companies that
sold internet service had relied on a rule connected to common
carrier protections mandating that phone companies had to sell
access to their networks at reasonable prices to competitors. One
of these companies, the California-based Brand X, disputed the
FCC's reclassification before the U.S. Court of Appeals for the
Ninth Circuit, which subsequently vacated the FCC's classification of cable broadband service as a Title I information service.[41]
Cable companies (like Comcast and Time Warner) would still be
required to sell access to their networks to independent ISPs
(like Earthlink and Brand X).

However, this decision was appealed and later overturned
on June 27, 2005, by a 6–3 Supreme Court decision in the case
of *National Cable & Telecommunications Association v. Brand X
Internet Services*. The decision favored the National Cable and
Telecommunications Association (NCTA), the principal trade
association of the cable television industry, by overturning the
earlier appellate court decision and affirming the FCC classification of cable broadband as an "information service" rather than a
"telecommunications service," thus exempting cable companies
from common carriage laws.[42]

Conservative justice Antonin Scalia's scathing dissent, in which he was joined by liberal justices David Souter and Ruth Bader Ginsburg, underscored the absurdity inherent in the argument that cable internet providers were not offering a telecommunications service: "This is a wonderful illustration of how an experienced agency can (with some assistance from credulous courts) turn statutory constraints into bureaucratic discretions. The main source of the Commission's regulatory authority over common carriers is Title II, but the Commission has rendered that inapplicable in this instance by concluding that the definition of 'telecommunications service' is ambiguous and does not (in its current view) apply to cable-modem service. . . . After all is said and done, after all the regulatory cant has been translated, and the smoke of agency expertise blown away, it remains perfectly clear that someone who sells cable-modem service is 'offering' telecommunications."[43]

Nonetheless, the FCC's decision to reclassify cable internet service as a Title I information service meant that cable internet providers did not have to share their infrastructure with competitors and that they did not have to abide by the principle of nondiscrimination. Weeks after the Supreme Court's *Brand X* decision, the FCC passed another rule that granted telephone companies the same power by reclassifying internet services provided over telephone networks such as DSL as an "information service." By removing these legal safeguards, the FCC

created the potential for ISPs to impose access restrictions to
nonpreferred content. Many public interest advocates pointed
out that these rulings imperiled the internet's open and non-
discriminatory nature by inaugurating a new class of potential
gatekeepers.

After the Supreme Court's fateful 2005 *Brand X* ruling,
Commissioner Copps and Commissioner Jonathan Adelstein
convinced their FCC colleagues to adopt the "Internet Policy
Statement," which upheld the basic rights of internet users to
access lawful content, run applications and services, connect
devices to the network, and benefit from competition among
different content and service providers.[44] While many saw this
move as a largely symbolic effort that was ultimately unenforceable, the policy statement nonetheless provided discursive
support for stronger net neutrality principles.

Meanwhile, a grassroots net neutrality movement was gaining
greater visibility, placing the issue on the political map for the
first time. Petition campaigns, Capitol Hill events, and media
coverage elevated net neutrality's profile within the nation's discourse. Open internet activists framed the debate as one around
nondiscrimination against content, drawing attention to net
neutrality's First Amendment implications as well as to democracy writ large. They also emphasized the internet's growing
centrality to everyday social and political life. Reformers argued
that the internet was too precious to treat as a profit-making

plaything of large ISPs. Instead, society should shield it from monopolies' commercial interests and the whims of the un-fettered market.

This position clashed with that of the Republican FCC commissioners, who saw net neutrality protections as at best unnecessary and at worst a heavy-handed government intrusion into the free marketplace. Former FCC commissioner Robert McDowell would later articulate the latter stance in a 2008 *Washington Post* op-ed, blasting the pro–net neutrality argument. He asserted that "engineers, not politicians or bureaucrats, should solve engineering problems."[45] This laissez-faire position seemed to carry the day at the FCC, but the net neutrality movement did not concede defeat.

A tipping point of sorts occurred when Comcast was caught throttling its subscribers' traffic in 2007. It all started with Robb Topolski, a mild-mannered network engineer who had a passion for barbershop quartet music—a folksy early-twentieth-century musical genre performed a cappella by four men or women dressed in flamboyant hats, shirts, and suspenders. That February, Topolski discovered that his ISP, Comcast, was blocking him from legally sharing his favorite (public domain) turn-of-the-century music through the peer-to-peer file-sharing client BitTorrent.[46] The Associated Press was able to independently verify that Comcast was clandestinely blocking BitTorrent and other peer-to-peer technologies by conducting a test: the AP attempted to download a text file of the King James Bible over Comcast's network, but it was blocked. Although they would later admit to manipulating their customers' access to BitTorrent, at the time Comcast vehemently denied any wrongdoing. Amid the height of the controversy, one Comcast spokesperson dissembled: "We're not blocking access to any application, and we don't throttle any traffic."[47]

What started with one intrepid internet user's frustration over not being able to share barbershop quartet music quickly transformed into a national scandal. Two media reform organizations, Free Press and Public Knowledge, brought a formal complaint against Comcast before the FCC, charging it with violating the 2005 Internet Policy Statement's prohibition against blocking users from accessing the legal internet content of their choice. As the controversy gained momentum, the FCC held a public hearing at Harvard Law School on February 25, 2008, to discuss the issue. However, this event turned into another PR disaster for Comcast. Having already been caught secretly blocking legal internet traffic, Comcast was exposed for trying to block public discussion of its conduct. Comcast admitted to hiring people off the streets to pack the auditorium and applaud Comcast's representatives on cue, leaving many activists and genuinely concerned citizens standing outside in the winter cold.[48]

Ultimately, in a 3–2 decision, Republican FCC chairman Kevin Martin broke ranks and joined the two Democratic commissioners in voting to sanction Comcast for unnecessarily meddling with its subscribers' traffic. In a blistering ruling, the FCC explained that BitTorrent had "become a competitive threat to cable operators such as Comcast because Internet users have the opportunity to view high-quality video with BitTorrent that they might otherwise watch (and pay for) on cable television."[49] Comcast proceeded to appeal the decision. In 2010, the U.S. Court of Appeals for the District of Columbia overturned the FCC's ruling on the basis that the FCC lacked "any statutorily mandated responsibility" to enforce network neutrality rules under Title I.[50]

The FCC was sent back to the drawing board to devise new net neutrality protections. There was a fierce debate over the best course of action, with some arguing that it was still possible to protect net neutrality under Title I, and others asserting that anything short of Title II was clearly doomed, as the court had just demonstrated. Even though the Democrats were now leading the agency and President Obama had campaigned on net neutrality, FCC chairman Julius Genachowski took the more conservative position and tried once again to secure net neutrality protections through Title I. Many pro–net neutrality advocates like Commissioner Copps disagreed with this decision. They instead called for stronger protections that were "effectively enforceable" and based on "the most solid possible legal foundation." Copps believed this required "reclassifying advanced telecommunications as a Title II telecommunications" and argued that the FCC "should just do it and get it over with."[51] However, the FCC voted to adopt the "Open Internet Order" under its limited Title I authority, which Copps, somewhat reluctantly, supported in the end.[52] While some felt that this was a pragmatic compromise by the FCC, critics maintained that relying on Title I authority was unenforceable and legally vulnerable.

These critics were proven correct after Verizon successfully sued the FCC to overturn even the relatively weak rules it had put in place. In January 2014, the U.S. Court of Appeals for the DC Circuit Court again thwarted the FCC when it threw out most of the 2010 Open Internet Order, which prevented internet service providers from blocking or unreasonably discriminating against the content, apps, and devices that use their network. The court ruled that the Open Internet Order imposed common carrier obligations on broadband internet access service providers, which was contrary to how the FCC had classified them.[53] Therefore, affirming what many critics had been saying all along, the DC Circuit Court declared that the FCC lacked the necessary regulatory authority under Title I to institute net neutrality.

Although it eliminated key net neutrality provisions, the court's decision was not a clear-cut defeat for net neutrality supporters because it rejected the 2010 Open Internet Order on narrow jurisdictional grounds rather than on the substance of the rules. In the eyes of reformers, it was more a defeat for a

weak FCC, pointing to a clear path toward establishing mean-
ingful net neutrality protections. The court decision shifted
responsibility back to the FCC to consider whether and how
to reintroduce net neutrality. The FCC was thus faced with a
choice: it could either adopt strong net neutrality protections by
reclassifying broadband internet as a Title II telecommunications provider or retreat to some version of "net neutrality lite."

A Temporary Triumph for Net Neutrality

It was unclear how the FCC would proceed. The industry-
friendly FCC chairman Julius Genachowski had stepped down
and the new FCC chairman, Tom Wheeler, was a former wireless and cable industry lobbyist. Having been on the job for just
a few months before being handed the case that would go on to
define his tenure, Wheeler initially pursued the more conservative option, deciding to tweak the rules that had just been thrown
out by the DC court instead of pursuing reclassification.[54] In
April 2014, he circulated a proposal to the FCC's four other
commissioners—two Democrats and two Republicans—that
allowed ISPs to create fast lanes for large edge providers like
Facebook, Google, and Netflix (and where there are fast lanes,
there must of course also be slow lanes). Chairman Wheeler's
proposal also allowed ISPs to offer fast lanes *exclusively* to one
competitor and not the other. Despite Wheeler's insistence that
his plan would "be tough" on ISPs, he essentially was offering

the same plan that cable and telephone companies had proposed for almost a decade and that had been consistently opposed by President Obama since he was a senator.[55]

Wheeler's proposal was roundly rebuffed by proponents of net neutrality and met with a barrage of activism. During the summer of 2014, millions of people swamped the FCC's website with comments demanding that it scrap Wheeler's proposal, eventually causing the website to crash. Battle for the Net, a coalition of media advocacy organizations and tech companies, coordinated an "Internet Slowdown Day" on September 10 in which forty thousand websites enjoined members of the public to call their elected representatives in support of strong net neutrality rules. Eventually this activism, which we discuss in greater detail in chapter 3, paid off.

On February 26, 2015, the FCC finally did what reformers had long been calling for—and what few had predicted was possible only months before—and reclassified broadband internet access as a telecommunications service, subject to common carrier rules. In one of the most important public interest decisions in American media policy history, the FCC, in a 3–2 party-line vote, reclassified broadband as a common carrier telecommunications service under Title II of the Communications Act.

Reformers hailed the Open Internet Order as a major, and all too rare, triumph in the historic struggle to define and defend the public interest. This ruling meant that the FCC now

possessed the regulatory authority to prevent ISPs from discriminating against (blocking or slowing down) online content or
creating fast and slow lanes based on whether content creators
could afford to pay up. This decision returned the internet to the
status of a telecommunications service under Title II, giving the
FCC the regulatory authority needed to prevent corporate gatekeeping. Copps, who was long gone from the commission by the
time the FCC finally passed strong net neutrality protections,
called the decision "the biggest FCC vote ever."[56]

The historic decision by the FCC to pass strong net neutrality
protections capped a thirteen-year struggle and was made possible by tremendous grassroots organizing and public protest.
It also served as an opening salvo for battles yet to come. Subsequent court challenges and efforts by the Republican-led Congress aimed to undercut the FCC's regulatory authority over
broadband internet. Potential litigants immediately lawyered up
for judicial review, and AT&T announced its intention to sue the
FCC even before its final decision had been made.[57] In addition
to the possibility that the courts might overturn net neutrality,
supporters feared that the FCC could simply reverse the Open
Internet Order in the future once a Republican won the presidency and majority control at the FCC. This concern would
indeed materialize.[58]

The long slog for net neutrality again drives home a key lesson from the history of media reform: if we fail to address core

structural problems like monopoly power and corporate control over our communication systems, important protections like net neutrality can be short-lived. Although reformers rightly heralded this decision as an all-too-rare boon for the public interest, this victory did not last long.

The Ongoing Death and Life of Net Neutrality

The improbable election of Donald Trump ushered back into power a corporate libertarian philosophy at the FCC.[59] Shortly after assuming office, Trump appointed a new FCC chairman, Ajit Pai, a former Verizon lawyer and staffer to conservative senators, who had been on the FCC for several years as a reliable party-line Republican vote. Pai pledged early on to use a "weed whacker" against regulations, with net neutrality his primary target.[60] Based on dubious arguments that ISPs had suffered financially under net neutrality and thus crippled investment in infrastructure, Pai unveiled his plan to hollow out net neutrality in early 2017.[61]

The path to repeal was marked by numerous undemocratic moves, especially regarding the FCC's public comment process. Concerned citizens submitted an unprecedented 20 million comments, the vast majority of which were in favor of retaining net neutrality.[62] At one point, the FCC's public comment system crashed, which Republican FCC commissioners attempted to blame on hackers. This was later exposed as a complete fabrication.[63] Although there was substantial evidence that there had been numerous irregularities, including millions of fraudulent comments, Chairman Pai refused to investigate these problems or postpone his decision to repeal net neutrality.

Despite these antics and the overwhelming public pressure against the move, the FCC ignored public opinion and plowed ahead. On December 14, 2017, in a dramatic moment—punctuated by an anonymous bomb threat right before the vote was scheduled—the FCC passed the Orwellian-sounding Restoring Internet Freedom Order, which eliminated core net neutrality protections by re-reclassifying broadband internet access as a Title I information service.[64] However, in some key respects, the FCC's decision went even further than most people had expected. Unlike previous Republican efforts to undermine strong net neutrality provisions, this initiative lacked any pretense that net neutrality was a principle worth saving at all—even in a weak, unenforceable way. As long as internet service providers publicly disclosed when they engage in blocking, throttling, or paid prioritization of internet traffic, Chairman Pai argued, the public interest was served.

Pai's rhetoric masked a deeper ideology—one focused on serving the interests of corporate oligopolies. This ideological commitment suggests that net neutrality was always about something far greater than who gets to manage the tubes and wires that comprise our internet. It was more about whether government has any serious regulatory authority over the internet whatsoever. By throwing out net neutrality protections, Pai essentially gave the telecom lobby exactly what it has wanted for years: freedom from regulatory oversight.

A World without Net Neutrality

In most policy decisions, certain interests benefit over others, and oftentimes specific groups are disproportionately harmed. So it is with the loss of net neutrality. Without this protection, independent media outlets and dissenting political voices that do not have the resources to compete in a pay-to-play media environment are particularly at risk. Moreover, without net neutrality protections, we can easily imagine ISPs now free to block or slow down content, and suppress views and news from certain outlets, especially economic competitors (which would hurt consumers) and those espousing anti-corporate politics (which would hurt democracy). Political groups opposed to concentrated corporate power—particularly the ascending social democratic movement in the United States—will likely suffer the most. Moreover, anyone involved in journalism or activism should be especially concerned about a post–net neutrality world where corporate censorship of speech is legally sanctioned. In the coming corporate libertarian internet landscape, those on the political left are disproportionately vulnerable.

Of course, industry representatives are quick to assure the

public that they will abide by net neutrality even in the absence of strong Title II protections. However, the fear that ISPs could block or throttle internet traffic is not just theoretical or speculative: there have been clear cases of net neutrality violations in the past. Before the FCC enacted the Open Internet Order in 2010, on numerous occasions ISPs censored communication on their networks that undermined or otherwise disparaged their business practices. Several warning signs of what a non-neutral network might look like appeared as early as 2004, when the North Carolina ISP Madison River blocked DSL customers from using its rival's (Vonage) VoIP telephony services. In 2005, the Canadian telecom corporation Telus, which is the second-largest telecommunications company in Canada, began blocking access to a server that hosted a website supporting a strike against the company during a labor dispute. In 2006, AOL Time Warner blocked a mass email campaign from its customers that opposed AOL's proposed tiered email system.[65]

Before the 2010 Open Internet Order, ISPs also acted as gatekeepers of political speech. In July 2005 Comcast was caught blocking its subscribers from receiving emails from After Downing Street, an organization that advocated ending the war in Iraq and impeaching President George W. Bush. As a result of Comcast's actions, After Downing Street's ability to set up time-sensitive calls with its members was significantly hampered, as were its plans to lobby Congress.[66] Just one month

later, another antiwar organization encountered difficulty com-
municating with its supporters over email. This time, Comcast,
Cox, and other ISPs blocked emails from MeetWithCindy, a
website created by Cindy Sheehan, an antiwar activist whose
son, U.S. Army Specialist Casey Sheehan, was killed in Iraq.[67]
Similarly, in August 2007 AT&T censored a live webcast of a
Pearl Jam concert when the rock group's lead singer Eddie
Vedder chanted: "George Bush, leave this world alone; George
Bush find yourself a home." While fans in the audience heard
Vedder's lyrics, AT&T's DSL customers heard sixteen seconds
of silence. Amid the ensuing controversy, Pearl Jam wrote on
its website: "AT&T's actions strike at the heart of the public's
concerns over the power that corporations have when it comes
to determining what the public sees and hears through communications media."[68]

More recently, net neutrality violations have continued to
abound on wireless internet networks. This is largely a result
of the tiered structure of the FCC's 2010 Open Internet Order,
which created a somewhat arbitrary regulatory distinction
between wireless ISPs and fixed-line ISPs, only the latter of
which was subject to net neutrality. In 2011, MetroPCS prevented its users from streaming video over its 4G network from
all websites except YouTube. From 2011 through 2013, AT&T,
T-Mobile, and Verizon blocked their users' access to Google
Wallet, which competed with their own mobile payment app,

the unfortunately named Isis.[69] In November 2018, even as the public outrage at ISPs was simmering, researchers revealed that Sprint had been throttling its users' connection to Skype since the beginning of the year. These are only the cases that were discovered and publicized. We will likely never know the true extent of the net neutrality violations that occurred in the past or the ones to come in the future.

As these examples show, the net neutrality debate has always been much more than a technical squabble over internet wires. It is part of a far larger power struggle over people's rights to express themselves politically and creatively and to access information of their choosing. It is also about the government's role in ensuring a level playing field and preventing corporate monopolies from abusing a socially vital infrastructure. At base, this debate is about the role of corporations—in our democracy and in our lives. For net neutrality advocates, this much is clear: the FCC's decision to scrap net neutrality protections will allow internet service providers like Comcast and Verizon to limit our access to online content, censor speech, and create pay-to-play "fast lanes" that will further amplify corporate power.

> *Some of the most important*
> *innovations in business in the*
> *last three decades have centered*
> *not on making the economy more*
> *efficient but on how better to*
> *ensure monopoly power or how*
> *better to circumvent government*
> *regulations intended to align so-*
> *cial returns and private rewards.*
> Joseph Stiglitz

TWO
THE BROADBAND CARTEL

After selecting Al Gore to be his running mate in the summer of 1992, presidential candidate Bill Clinton incorporated much of Gore's technology policy agenda into his platform. Based on one of Gore's most ambitious ideas, Clinton called for building an "information super-highway" through a massive New Deal–style public works program. The information superhighway was conceived of as a public network that would be constructed by the government and operated by the private sector, with substantial regulation and oversight by the public sector.[1] Initially, this was a Keynesian social democratic program designed to stimulate demand during a time of economic malaise

in the early 1990s, while also providing an important public
good. However, after encountering vociferous opposition from
Wall Street—particularly long-distance telephone companies—
the administration quickly changed course and dropped
references to public works and public investment in its subsequent proposals. The Clinton administration ultimately argued
that "the private sector should lead" in the development of
America's internet infrastructure and that "innovation, expanded services, broader participation, and lower prices will
arise in a market-driven arena, not in an environment that
operates as a regulated industry."[2]

This episode is emblematic of a shift from a Keynesian to a
neoliberal or corporate libertarian public policy paradigm that
privileges the interests of media corporations over the public
good. This chapter shows how this commercial logic has been
instrumental to the growth of monopoly power in the broadband
industry over the last twenty years. We argue that the repeal of
net neutrality is a symptom of the monopolistic structure of the
broadband industry, particularly the immense market power
wielded by the likes of Comcast, Verizon, and Charter.

Access Denied

In the 1990s, many commentators eagerly prophesied that the
arrival of the internet signaled the imminent death of legacy
telephone and cable companies. They speculated that internet-

based applications such as VoIP (voice over IP) would replace the need for wired telephone service and that streaming online video would replace cable television amid an endless cycle of creative destruction that would be unleashed by the internet. "The rise of Skype and other VoIP services means nothing less than the death of the traditional telephone business, established over a century ago," an article in the *Economist* confidently declared.[3] What these prognostications did not account for, however, was that the digital revolution would transpire over the wires and cables of the very industries that were supposed to be disrupted: the internet itself was laid over the existing telecommunications infrastructure. The cable and telephone monopolies of the twentieth century would survive, and eventually thrive, in the digital era through their ownership of the networks that bring internet connectivity to home and business subscribers.

Though incumbent telephone and cable companies ran lines into most homes in the United States, it took a significant political struggle for these companies to become the country's dominant internet service providers. The 1996 Telecommunications Act's open-access requirement led to a brief period of fierce competition between incumbent telephone companies and independent internet service providers. By forcing telephone monopolies to lease their lines to independent ISPs, open access undermined the ability of telephone monopolies to conquer the market for internet access by closing their lines to potential competitors. As former FCC chairman William Kennard noted, "Introducing competition in monopoly markets requires consistent pro-competition intervention by the government. . . . *This thought that if the government gets out of the way, competition will somehow spontaneously bloom, I just don't get it.*"[4]

Indeed, active government policy created the conditions necessary for a vibrant, competitive market for internet access to succeed by placing restraints on the private property rights of the telcos. Thousands of new independent ISPs, such as AOL and Earthlink, were established and competed by offering dial-up or DSL internet service over incumbent telephone companies' copper telephone networks. By 1998, 92 percent of the U.S. population had the ability to choose between seven or more internet service providers just through their telephone line.[5] Net neutrality advocates valued this burgeoning competition in the ISP market not only for its effect on quality of service and prices but also for its ability to prevent discrimination and other forms of predatory behavior by the incumbents. In a robust market for internet service, open-access advocates reasoned, consumers can punish ISPs that engage in discriminatory activity simply by switching providers. The FCC's own research confirmed that open access networks deliver cheaper, better service courtesy of competition.[6]

However, this competitive market for internet service did not last long. Big telephone companies like AT&T and Sprint were loath to rent out their wires to independent ISPs at government-regulated rates that, they argued, were below what they would demand in commercial negotiations. Large cable companies like Comcast and Time Warner feared that they too would be reclassified as Title II common carriers and forced to allow independent ISPs to use their infrastructure. In the aftermath of the 1996 Telecommunications Act, telephone and cable corporations spent millions of dollars lobbying and litigating to repeal open access while perpetually underinvesting in their network infrastructure. As telecommunications scholar Rob Frieden observes, network operators "appeared more intent on competing in the courtroom than in the marketplace."[7]

Eventually, as a result of the Supreme Court's *Brand X* decision, most independent ISPs went out of business. Incumbent ISPs either closed their wires to the independents or imposed draconian conditions for leasing access to their networks that effectively prevented independent ISPs from competing against them. Time Warner, for instance, demanded that any independent ISP that wanted to continue to provide internet service over its network had to give Time Warner 75 percent of its subscriber revenues and 25 percent of any ancillary revenues.[8] Whereas dozens of ISPs could provide internet access over a single copper telephone line in the 1990s, today most telephone, cable, or fiber-optic lines are exclusive to one ISP.

The defeat of open access created enormous barriers to

competitive entry in the broadband market.[9] In the absence of open access, independent ISPs that wish to challenge the broadband oligopoly are often forced to expend large amounts of capital to "overbuild"—that is, build new, redundant physical networks in cities and towns that are already served by a high-speed internet provider. Potential challengers to incumbent ISPs thus face enormous up-front construction costs that are only slowly recouped over a long period, provided they can outcompete the incumbent ISP for customers. Google's failure in 2016 to make Google Fiber into a nationwide internet service demonstrates just how hard it is even for the most deep-pocketed, long-term-oriented companies to break into the broadband market by building new facilities rather than by sharing existing ones.

Invoking phrases such as "forced access," "forced entry," and "infrastructure socialism," opponents of open access framed their opposition in libertarian terms, as an unwarranted intrusion on the private property rights of internet service providers.[10] In 2003, Republican FCC commissioner Michael Powell inveighed: "When someone advocates regulatory regimes for broadband that look like, smell like, feel like common carriage, scream at them! They will almost always suggest that it is just a 'light touch.' Demand to see the size of the hand that is going to lay its finger on the market. Insist on knowing where it all stops."[11] In a more measured critique of open access, in the Supreme Court's 2004 *Verizon Communications v. Trinko* decision—a case in which independent ISPs accused Verizon of denying them access to Verizon's network—conservative justice Antonin Scalia admonished that "enforced sharing also requires antitrust courts to act as central planners, identifying the proper price, quantity, and other terms of dealing—a role for which they are ill-suited."[12]

In the libertarian discourse of "forced access," the market is the fount of liberty and the state is an instrument of unjust hierarchy, centralization, and coercion. The irony here is that open access created a much more competitive, decentralized market for internet service in the United States than the closed access model has. By insisting that the property rights of incumbent ISPs were inviolable and that they had no obligation to share their infrastructure with independent ISPs, corporate libertarians sanctioned the development of an oligopolistic market for internet access. Moreover, although opposition to open access was often registered in anti-statist terms, as heavy-handed legislation imposed by "central planners," the dominance of corporations like Comcast, Verizon, and AT&T is due in part to the historic role played by the government in shaping cable and telecommunications markets throughout the twentieth century. Indeed, today's ISP empires are the offspring either of government-granted monopoly licenses for cable television systems or the state-protected Bell system of the twentieth century, which legally enshrined limits on competitive entry in the telecommunications market.

The erasure of the government's critical role in the development of telecommunications technologies and markets implicitly positions large corporations as the lone engine of technological progress and miscasts the American state as an impediment to economic development. In fact, beyond the massive subsidies that we discussed earlier, the internet itself would have never developed during the dial-up era without common carrier laws. This was true for at least two reasons. First, Title II open access provisions created a vibrant market for internet access across the Unites States, which greatly aided in broadening internet adoption in the late 1990s and early 2000s. Second, common carrier rules forced telecom providers to allow their customers to use equipment and attach devices of their choice—including answering machines and fax machines—to their networks. The FCC's landmark *Carterfone* decision in 1968 further established this protection by requiring AT&T and other telcos to allow interconnection of third-party equipment to their telephone network as long as it did not interfere with network operations.[13] The *Carterfone* decision paved the way for the widespread adoption of a particularly important device: the modem. Prior to the ruling, AT&T was able to leverage its ownership of the nation's telephone networks into a near monopoly in the telephone equipment market by preventing equipment manufactured by other companies from connecting to its network.[14] While the policy roots of the internet's ascendance are often omitted in popular origin narratives, they demonstrate that it was government— and not only the so-called free market—that drove the internet's creation and expansion.

The War That Was Not Waged

In neoclassical economic thought, power is, by definition, absent from free market economies. As the Chicago School economist George J. Stigler says: "The essence of perfect competition is . . . the utter dispersion of power." Stigler adds that power is "annihilated . . . just as a gallon of water is effectively annihilated if it is spread over a thousand acres."[15] Although contemporary adherents of neoclassical economics fetishize the virtue of unfettered markets, the deregulation of the telecommunication and cable industries in the name of boosting competition has, in practice, led to oligopoly and conglomeration.

The 1996 Telecommunications Act was supposed to unleash a Hobbesian "war of all against all" throughout the entire telecommunications industry.[16] Over a decade in the making, the legislation was the handiwork of the "Gingrich class" of Republicans that were swept into power during the 1994 midterm elections, key members of the Clinton administration including Vice President Al Gore, and the thousands of industry lobbyists

who were privately invited by policymakers to help craft the bill.[17]
Relaxing ownership restrictions and other regulations, policymakers argued, would result in local telephone companies (such
as Verizon and Bell Atlantic), long-distance providers (such as
AT&T and MCI), and cable companies all using their respective
infrastructure to invade one another's traditional bailiwicks and
compete for market share. The hype was that the cable and
telephone incumbents would be joined by satellite, wireless, and
even electric companies ("broadband over powerline") in offering internet access to consumers.

However, the 1996 Telecommunications Act spawned not
cutthroat competition between telecommunications firms but a
genteel détente between the largest cable and telephone companies. Instead of promoting ubiquitous competition, the Telecommunications Act precipitated what Schwartzman, Leanza, and
Feld describe as "the greatest wave of media consolidation in history."[18] Given the opportunity to compete on one another's turf,
the eight regional Baby Bells that were created from the breakup
of Ma Bell in 1984 instead opted to merge back together. Southwestern Bell Corporation (SBC) bought Pacific Telesis in 1997,
Ameritech in 1999, AT&T in 2005 (Southwestern subsequently
changed its name to AT&T and took on its branding), and Bell
South in 2006. In 1997, Bell Atlantic and NYNEX merged in
what was at the time the second-largest merger in American
corporate history, changing the company's name to Verizon in

2000 after acquiring GTE. Under the guise of liberalization, the horizontal integration of the former Baby Bells into AT&T and Verizon has created a highly concentrated wireless broadband market: together, these two companies account for more than two-thirds of the mobile wireless subscriptions in the United States.[19] As Susan Crawford notes, "Instead of the twentieth century's Ma Bell, we now have Ma Cell."[20] Though both exert considerable market power, the main difference is that "Ma Cell" is exempt from the common carrier regulations that had applied to Ma Bell for decades.

Like the telephone industry, the cable industry has consolidated from dozens of regional players to just a handful of giants. Two decades of mergers and acquisitions have left Comcast and Charter as the two largest broadband providers in the country. Together, these two companies account for more than three-quarters of the cable internet market and over half of the total wired broadband market.[21] The duopolies' share of the broadband internet market is increasing as customers transition away from the slower DSL services provided by Verizon, AT&T, and other incumbent telephone companies to faster, more reliable cable internet. Thus, horizontal integration in both the telephone and cable industries has led to a highly concentrated broadband market in which a dwindling number of firms exercise an increasingly large amount of control over the provision of internet services.

Yet, horizontal mergers have proceeded apace, in part because many pro-industry regulators came to embrace a hollowed-out standard of "competition" that is quite compatible with monopoly. Competition is conceived of principally as a competition between different technologies—cable, DSL, wireless, and so forth—rather than as a competition between companies. The presence of oligopolistic power in the market for cable broadband is tolerated on the basis that Comcast's and Charter's reign is only transitory and that the next technological breakthrough will introduce new competition to the broadband market. Thus, the *theoretical* possibility of competition in the future suffices as a reason to tolerate the lack of *actual* competition in the present. As Tim Wu puts it, the George W. Bush administration's approach to internet policy "tended to agree that competition didn't necessarily require that there be any extant competitors."[22]

Corporate libertarian approaches to internet policy therefore obscure the market power of dominant internet service providers, turning a normative political question about the control that these companies wield over our nation's communications infrastructure into a technological one. Market concentration is a problem that can be solved not through political means—by passing antitrust legislation, implementing more aggressive ownership caps, and so forth—but through technological innovation. FCC chairman Ajit Pai reasons, "I want all of these technologies to compete, but you won't have a fair chance of getting those smaller competitive entrants in if you heavily regulate this marketplace to begin with."[23]

As we shall see, there are many contradictions within this discourse. Oftentimes, it is the very policymakers espousing such libertarian positions who seek to institute regulations that benefit market incumbents. They are quite comfortable with regulations that help large corporations maximize profits (for example, intellectual property law). Even the very notion of regulation itself is flawed. Why is it that throwing out net neutrality amounts to "deregulation"? In many ways, such policy changes are actually a form of *re-regulation*—regulation along corporate libertarian lines that determines what sites we are allowed to visit and on what terms. To call this deregulation is a gross misnomer.

From Oligopoly to Cartel

When Adam Smith wrote that "people of the same trade seldom meet together, even for merriment and diversion, but the conversation ends in a conspiracy against the public, or in some contrivance to raise prices," he was referring to the collusive practices between industrial capitalists in the late eighteenth century, but he might as well have been describing the machinations of the telecommunications industry today.[24] In a competitive market for internet access, ISPs would have to drop their prices, spend more money to upgrade their infrastructure, and improve their services in order to retain or attract customers.

Instead, over the last twenty years, Comcast, Charter, Verizon, and AT&T have worked together to parcel the broadband market into private fiefdoms that are liberated from both the discipline of the market and government oversight.

According to the economist William Shephard, a "tight oligopoly" exists when the four leading firms in an industry capture 60 percent to 100 percent of a market: Comcast, Charter, Verizon, and AT&T currently account for 76 percent of the internet subscriptions in the United States (see table 1).[25] However, collaboration between these companies makes the broadband market even *less* competitive than might be expected within a highly concentrated, oligopolistic market. Indeed, Comcast, Charter, Verizon, and AT&T work together to assert their collective control over the broadband internet market, operating more as a cartel than as competitors.[26] In the economics literature, a cartel generally refers to collusive agreements between nominally independent firms within an industry to coordinate production and distribution. Like the cartels of the railroad industry during the late nineteenth century and the Organization of the Petroleum Exporting Countries (OPEC) today, the broadband cartel drives prices up by restricting output, deterring competition emanating from outside the cartel, and granting members control over different geographic markets.

Comcast, Charter, Verizon, and AT&T all have a considerable

Table 1. Market share of major broadband ISPs, Q2 2018

Broadband provider	Number of household subscriptions (in millions)	Percent of total
Comcast	26.5	27.3
Charter	24.6	25.4
AT&T	15.8	16.2
Verizon	7	7.2
All other major ISPs	23.2	23.9

share of the wired broadband market at the national level but deliberately avoid competing with one another for customers at the point of sale. During Comcast's failed acquisition of Time Warner Cable in 2014, Comcast's vice president David Cohen attempted to assuage public concerns that the merger would reduce competition: "Despite claims by certain commenters, Comcast and TWC have never had plans to expand into each other's territory . . . no incumbent cable operator ever has."[27] In other words, the proposed merger would not reduce competition because competition between the big cable ISPs was already scarce to begin with. Comcast and Charter (which bought Time Warner Cable in 2016) have a combined territory covering about 211 million people across the country. Yet the companies' overlapping service territory covers only 1.5 million people.[28] In effect, the cable duopoly has agreed to a nonaggression pact.

The members of the broadband cartel have also worked together to minimize their exposure to market pressures through a process called "clustering." Clustering involves creating regional monopolies through the acquisition of smaller companies within the regional monopolist's sphere of control (such as Comcast's partial purchase of the Pennsylvania-based Adelphia cable company in 2006) and "swapping" customers with one another to carve out larger, more geographically contiguous, and less competitive markets. The most notorious wave of clustering occurred in the summer of 1997, during which the main cable operators pursued customer swaps and partnerships that put all but four markets in the hands of a single operator. Leo Hindery Jr., the former president of Tele-Communications, Inc., affectionately referred to this period as the "summer of love."[29] More recently, in 2014 Comcast swapped 1.6 million of its customers in southern and midwestern states to Charter for 1.6 million of the latter's subscribers in Boston, Atlanta, and parts of California.[30]

While clustering has been a financial boon for the big cable and telecommunications companies over the years, it has been a burden for everyone else. Potential overbuilders have a much harder time breaking into highly protected clustered markets. Without the threat of independent overbuilders to act as a constraint on Big Cable and Big Telecom, customers living in clustered markets encounter much higher rates for internet service.[31]

For their part, AT&T and Verizon have largely ceded the wired broadband market to the cable companies. In 2004, Verizon embarked on an ambitious (and expensive) plan to roll out high-speed fiber-optic lines across the country. Although Verizon FiOS is faster and more reliable than cable internet, in 2010 Verizon announced that it was suspending the build-out of FiOS into new cities and towns.[32] Digging up and replacing their old copper telephone wires with high-speed fiber-optic cables involved hefty capital expenditures that Wall Street despised. Instead of competing with the cable firms in the wired broadband market, Verizon and AT&T decided to collaborate with them. The major development occurred in 2011 when Verizon bought $3.6 billion worth of wireless spectrum from Comcast and Time Warner Cable. As part of this complex deal, Verizon, Time Warner Cable, and Comcast agreed to cross-promote and sell one another's services. Even as Verizon maintained its FiOS internet network, its own website boasted that Comcast offered "the fastest Internet service in the nation."[33] These are the actions not of fierce competitors but of a cartel intent on abusing its market power.

Because of the extensive coordination between Comcast, Charter, Verizon, and AT&T, Americans are left with little choice when it comes to selecting an internet service provider. According to the FCC's most recent "Internet Access Services" report—

and these reports are notorious for overstating the amount of competition in the residential broadband market—42 percent of Americans have access to one or fewer broadband providers. These are effectively captive markets in which customers are not able to "vote with their wallets" if they are dissatisfied with their ISP. Of the remaining internet users who do not live in a captive market, most have a choice between just two ISPs, often one cable and one phone provider.[34]

If the FCC implemented the Democrat-appointed commissioner Jessica Rosenworcel's proposal to raise the agency's broadband speed standard from twenty-five to one hundred megabits per second (Mbps), only 15 percent of the country would have access to more than one provider. Twenty-five Mbps is scarcely enough bandwidth to sustain even current levels of data usage, let alone the bandwidth that will be needed in the near future as applications become even more data intensive. For example, a single high-definition Netflix stream can eat a twenty-five Mbps connection by itself. The demand for bandwidth is further strained by the growing number of devices that internet users connect to their network. In 2017, Pew Research found that a regular household in the United States has five devices connected to its home network, and that 18 percent of households have more than ten, including computers, smartphones, gaming devices, tablets, streaming media players such as Roku, and smart-home technologies.[35]

Net Neutrality as an Oligopoly Problem

The broadband internet access market has failed consumers but handsomely rewarded the broadband cartel. Most Americans pay more money to their internet service provider for slower connections than their global counterparts. Nationwide, the average cost for broadband internet is $61.07 a month.[36] By comparison, a one-hundred Mbps broadband connection in Sweden and Norway costs between $10 and $20 less than a much slower internet plan in the United States.[37] Residents of South Korea, Japan, Singapore, and Hong Kong can subscribe to a gigabit (one thousand Mbps) internet connection for between $30 and $50 a month.[38]

Some argue that Americans pay more for internet service because ISPs have to serve a population that is spread out over a vast geographic area. However, the cost of internet access is high even in densely populated urban areas of the United States. The average monthly price for an internet plan ranging in speed from twenty-five to fifty Mbps is $64.95 in New York City, $66.66 in Washington, DC, and $69.98 in Los Angeles. (These figures actually understate how much Americans pay for broadband internet, as they do not include the hidden fees and spurious surcharges that are tacked onto customers' bills.) Meanwhile, a twenty-five- to fifty-Mbps internet connection costs $24.77 in London, $35.50 in Paris, and $39.48 in Tokyo.[39] In fact, broadband internet access is more expensive in the United States than

63

it is in every other country that belongs to the Organisation for Economic Co-operation and Development (OECD), with the lone exception of Mexico.[40] What these countries have in common is that they have implemented some form of open access. What makes America exceptional is that it has not. In stark contrast to the United States, since 2001 the European Union has mandated that incumbents share their network infrastructure with competitors, which has largely kept internet prices in check.[41] Most other OECD countries outside of the European Union have implemented open access policies as well.

The premium that American consumers pay for internet access has been siphoned off into the coffers of Comcast, Verizon, and Wall Street. In the absence of robust policy to encourage competition or strong government price regulation, the broadband cartel is able to command "monopoly rents," super-profits from their customers that are well in excess of what competitive market conditions would otherwise tolerate. The desire of the broadband cartel to repeal net neutrality is an effort to capture yet another source of monopoly rents: by privileging certain kinds of internet traffic over others, ISPs can pressure internet users and content providers to hand over even more money.

High prices, slow speeds, and the segregation of internet traffic into fast and slow lanes are all consequences of the immense market power of the broadband cartel. Constrained neither by competition nor government oversight, the cartel has established enormous leverage over internet users and online content providers, which it fully intends to use. During oral arguments in *Verizon v. FCC* in 2013, the presiding judges asked Verizon counsel Helgi Walker whether Verizon would favor some preferred services, content, or websites in the absence of net neutrality. Walker responded: "I'm authorized to state from my client today that but for these rules we would be exploring those types of arrangements."[42]

Sans net neutrality, it is now legally possible for ISPs to charge their customers to get high-quality Netflix or Hulu video streaming or to access popular social media platforms such as Facebook. However, it is far more likely that ISPs will demand their pound of flesh directly from the websites themselves. In this "pay-to-play" post–net neutrality digital landscape, some of the costs of paid prioritization will be borne by particular websites and services—at least the ones that are willing and able to pay for a fast lane—but some of the costs will eventually be passed on to internet users. Internet users will pay their broadband providers monopoly rent twice: first directly, in the form of an inflated monthly bill for their internet subscription, and second indirectly, through the higher prices certain websites will charge consumers to access their content, which will then be routed back to the ISPs.

The vertical integration of the broadband cartel into internet content and applications has further increased the incentive for

ISPs to engage in traffic discrimination. Indeed, Comcast owns NBCUniversal and DreamWorks Pictures and has made large investments in online content companies such as Vox Media and BuzzFeed; Verizon owns Yahoo!, AOL, Tumblr, and the *Huffington Post;* and AT&T owns HBO, Warner Bros., and DirecTV and has a stake in Hulu. This sets up a major conflict of interest: these media empires both operate as a conduit of data, information, and content and are the owners of much of the content that flows over the wires in their market area. The broadband cartel has every financial motivation to undermine rival content producers by deprioritizing their traffic.

Trickle-Down Broadband

From Bill Clinton to Ajit Pai, America's internet policy over the last twenty-five years has been guided by an abiding faith that free markets, private sector innovation, and "light-touch" government regulation will deliver us from our contentious analog past to our high-tech, seamless digital future. Of course, this disposition is not unique to debates about internet policy; it springs from the broader ideological environment within which these debates are ensconced. Indeed, this approach to internet policy is consistent with a neoliberal framework, redolent of the "trickle-down" economic theory espoused by Ronald Reagan and his adviser Arthur Laffer during the 1980s. The Reagan administration invoked trickle-down economics to justify all manner of legislation benefiting the wealthy and powerful on the basis that the economic gains accrued by the 1 percent would, eventually, reach far and wide in society.

Contemporary opposition to net neutrality is similarly premised on reducing the public interest to the welfare of big internet service providers. In the corporate libertarian paradigm, net neutrality is seen as a barrier to corporate investment in broadband deployment and technological innovation. The argument implies that the public will ultimately be better off by allowing the broadband cartel to turn the open internet into a tiered, pay-to-play service. According to opponents of net neutrality, the extra profits that ISPs harvest from a non-neutral internet will "trickle down" to internet users as ISPs lower their cost of service and invest more money into modernizing their network infrastructure.

By its own logic, the trickle-down theory of broadband deployment does not withstand serious scrutiny. The broadband cartel does not lack money for infrastructure investment; its members have been reaping monopoly profits for decades and are more than capable of paying for necessary infrastructure upgrades several times over. Indeed, experts estimate that America's major ISPs generate comically high profit margins, upwards of 80 percent a year on high-speed internet services.[43]

These monopoly profits have not led to a deluge of spending on next-generation broadband infrastructure: comparative capital investments in telecommunication networks in the United

States and European Union currently stand at similar levels.[44]
Instead, the broadband cartel uses its largesse to line the pockets
of corporate executives and large institutional investors on Wall
Street. In 2017, Charter spent $13.2 billion on stock buybacks—
a scheme that enriches a company's shareholders by artificially
inflating the value of their stock.[45] That same year, Comcast also
announced $5 billion in stock buybacks in addition to a massive
21 percent increase in its annual dividend worth another $5
billion.[46]

America's internet infrastructure suffers because giant ISPs
tend to hoard their wealth rather than invest it, not because they
are overburdened by public interest regulations such as net
neutrality. In fact, under oligopolistic market conditions, repealing net neutrality creates a perverse incentive for ISPs *not* to
invest in network upgrades. Instead of spending money on
modernizing their network to meet the ever-growing demand
for bandwidth, paid prioritization allows ISPs to auction off the
scarce amount of bandwidth made available by their existing,
aging infrastructure to those willing to pay the most for it.

Yet even if it were true that net neutrality hampered broadband investment, it would still be a principle worth fighting for.
As the next chapter will argue, net neutrality is a cornerstone of
democracy in the digital age that will be won or lost by democratic actions and movements, not by the investment decisions
of the broadband cartel.

THREE

**THE MAKING OF
A MOVEMENT**

When Tim Wu coined the term *network neutrality* in 2002, the concept was less a fully formed political demand than a proposal for managing network traffic. Yet it was the term that open internet activists—much to their initial chagrin—would be stuck with. Joshua Breitbart lamented in 2006, "Progressives trying to protect the Internet from corporate hijacking have once again shot themselves in the foot by trying to rally people around 'net neutrality.' Only a Democrat would think people could get excited about neutrality. What's the opposite of 'neutral'? Non-neutral . . . Partisan . . . In gear . . . ?" Arianna Huffington, co-founder of the liberal blog the *Huffington Post*, asserted that the term net neutrality was akin to "marketing death" and that the idea desperately needed to be rebranded.[1] For those concerned about the fate of the open internet in the mid-2000s, "net neutrality" was a soporific expression that only a network engineer or policy wonk could love.

This anxiety over the phrase pointed toward a much more substantive fear: that net neutrality would remain an arcane, technocratic debate between, on the one hand, a small vanguard of technologists and media activists and, on the other, a large army of handsomely paid lobbyists for the telecom and cable industries. This concern was well founded, at least initially. According to a 2006 poll, only 7 percent of Americans had even heard about net neutrality.[2]

However, over the next decade, millions of Americans came to rally behind the cause of net neutrality. At times, the public's support for net neutrality has become so widespread that policymakers and other Washington insiders have openly pined for the days when they could make critical decisions about the future of the internet without so much public scrutiny. One particularly exemplary report in this regard was published by the industry-funded Information Technology and Innovation Foundation (ITIF) in 2015, in which the authors wistfully reminisced: "There was a time when technology policy was a game of 'inside baseball' played mostly by wonks from government agencies, legislative committees, think tanks, and the business community." For these policy elites, rational public policy can come about

only in the absence of the demos. But now, thanks to widespread
mobilization around policy issues such as net neutrality and
SOPA/PIPA (Stop Online Piracy Act / Protect Intellectual Property Act), the barbarians are at the proverbial gates: "Tech policy
debates now are increasingly likely to be shaped by angry, populist uprisings."[3]

Over the last fifteen years, net neutrality has sometimes been
a marginal issue on the public agenda. During these relatively
quiet periods, powerful actors on both sides of the debate, including ISPs, large internet companies, lobbying groups, unions,
and advocacy organizations, maneuver behind the scenes to
influence policymakers. These periods generally favor corporate
opponents of net neutrality, who prefer to conduct their affairs
outside of public purview. However, there have been a number
of flash points scattered throughout the duration of the net
neutrality battle—usually in anticipation of or in response to
an FCC decision—that give rise to heightened public interest
and activism.

This chapter examines four key phases of net neutrality
activism: the initial period of mobilization in 2006, the fallout
from the Google-Verizon net neutrality compromise in 2010,
the activism that followed the repeal of net neutrality rules by
a federal appeals court in 2014, and the push back against the
FCC's decision to repeal net neutrality in the aftermath of
Donald Trump's election. We pay particular attention to the

ways that activists have broken the net neutrality debate out of the narrow confines of elite institutions—including official government policymaking bodies, corporations, and think tanks—and transformed the issue into an object of mass democratic political action. Net neutrality activism is not only about securing more just and equitable policy outcomes—it is also about democratizing the policymaking process itself.

Strange Bedfellows

Net neutrality emerged amid the decline of the open-access movement. Just months after the Supreme Court's 2005 *Brand X* decision signaled the death knell of open access, SBC's CEO Ed Whitacre hinted that he expected internet companies like Google and Yahoo! to pay SBC for bringing their content into the homes of his company's subscribers: "What they would like to do is use my pipes for free, but I ain't going to let them do that because we have spent this capital and we have to have a return on it."[4] Whitacre's brazen remarks affirmed the worst fears of media activists: that internet service providers were planning to create a tiered, pay-to-play internet. It was the first public attempt by ISPs to "double-dip" by charging both their subscribers and internet content providers to access each other. This catalyzed many politicians and media activists to redouble their efforts to rein in the broadband cartel. Beginning with the introduction of the Internet Freedom and Non-discrimination Act (S. 2360) by

Senator Ron Wyden (D-Oregon) on March 2, 2006, a flurry of
net neutrality legislation was proposed in both the Senate and
the House of Representatives. Much weaker proposals by congressional Republicans and pro-telecom Democrats would wend
their way through Congress as well, most notably the Communications Opportunity Promotion and Enhancement (COPE) Act.

The driving force behind the burgeoning net neutrality movement was Free Press, a media reform organization founded in
2003 by media scholar Robert McChesney, progressive journalist
John Nichols, and veteran activist Josh Silver, who served as the
first president and CEO of the organization.[5] Free Press was the
central organizing body behind the Save the Internet coalition,
which comprised over eight hundred pro–net neutrality groups.
Free Press aggressively fought to assemble a politically diverse
left-right coalition that included liberal groups such as MoveOn
.org, Feminist Majority, and the American Civil Liberties Union
as well as conservative organizations such as the Christian
Coalition of America, the American Patriot Legion, and Gun
Owners of America.

These groups tended to frame net neutrality primarily as a
free speech issue, as a way to prevent ISPs from acting as gatekeepers of the online public sphere. "Internet freedom" became
a rallying cry for the nascent movement. MoveOn warned its
members, "Internet freedom is under attack as Congress pushes
a law that would give companies like AT&T the power to control

what you do online."[6] On the other side of the political spectrum, Roberta Combs, president of the Christian Coalition of America, rhetorically asked: "What if a cable company with a pro-choice Board of Directors decides that it doesn't like a pro-life organization using its high-speed network to encourage pro-life activities? Under the new rules, they could slow down the pro-life web site, harming their ability to communicate with other pro-lifers—and it would be legal."[7]

The Save the Internet coalition also included large internet-based corporations such as Google, Amazon, and eBay. In contrast to many of the public interest organizations that participated in the Save the Internet coalition, corporations like Google foregrounded the ability of ISPs to suffocate innovation and entrepreneurship. The threat posed by ISPs to democratic speech rights was usually of secondary concern to them. Although these companies indulged the free speech rhetoric of their coalition partners, their primary motivation for supporting net neutrality was every bit as self-interested as the ISPs' motivation for opposing it. The difference was that companies like Google and Amazon were initially perceived by many supporters of net neutrality as fairly benign—or even benevolent—actors compared to Comcast or AT&T.

The Save the Internet coalition's corporate-activist alliance hinged on the understanding that the financial interest of large internet companies in net neutrality was broadly in harmony with the public's interest. Some leading activists sought to appeal to diverse coalition members—including industry partners—by emphasizing how the loss of net neutrality might prevent the next Google or eBay from having a fair chance at getting started online.[8] During this early phase of the net neutrality battle, it seemed politically beneficial for activists to couch some of their rhetoric in pro-business language and to have a corporate titan or two on their side. Though large corporations such as Google did not fund Save the Internet, their participation in the coalition did confer a degree of political legitimacy to its grassroots coalition partners.

Within just a few months, activists began to transform net neutrality from an abstruse, technocratic debate into a cause with broad, even populist, appeal. Populism brings diverse groups together by emphasizing the binary opposition of "the people" to a common enemy, in this case the large, commercial internet service providers and the politicians who do their bidding in Washington.[9] The populist understanding of net neutrality that was fashioned during this early period of activism in 2006 focused not on the technical minutiae involved in the net neutrality debate but on the fundamental antagonism between ISPs and the digital public—broadly construed to include not only ordinary internet users but also internet companies like Google. For example, in December 2006 Save the Internet released a four-minute viral video on YouTube entitled *Indepen-*

dence Day. The narrator defines net neutrality as a sort of defense of the populist "everyman." "Whether it's . . . everyday citizens or a business tycoon: everybody's website gets the same speed and quality. That's called net neutrality." Later in the video, as the narrator explains how ISPs are plotting to roll back net neutrality, flying saucers bearing the corporate logos of Comcast, Verizon, and AT&T hover around on the screen and shoot laser beams at the United States Capitol Building before moving on to attack various state legislatures. These internet service providers are depicted not only as enemies of American democracy but as external to the body politic—literally alien to it.[10]

Perhaps the single most important turning point of the 2006 net neutrality debate was the result of an error committed by Alaskan senator Ted Stevens—a blustering, crotchety lifelong politician who, as chairman of the Senate's Committee on Commerce, Science, and Transportation wielded more influence over internet policy than perhaps anybody else in Congress at the time. In June 2006, Stevens gave a rambling eleven-minute speech against net neutrality on the Senate floor: "I just the other day got an internet [that] was sent by my staff at ten o'clock in the morning on Friday, and I just got it yesterday! Why?!" Stevens punctuated his wandering tirade with a now-infamous metaphor: "The internet is not something you just dump something on. It's not a big truck. It's, it's a series of tubes!"[11]

Stevens's remark that the internet was a "series of tubes" was

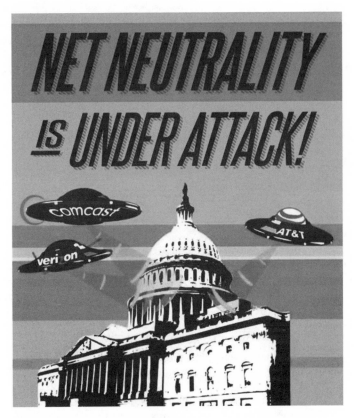

Poster, based on Save the Internet's 2006 video *Independence Day*, showing three of America's largest internet service providers attacking the United States Capitol Building. (Courtesy of Free Press.)

a gift to satirists and supporters of net neutrality alike. Within days of the senator's gaffe, millions of citizens learned about the public benefits of net neutrality. The audio clip of his comments ricocheted throughout the blogosphere, turning Stevens into an object of merciless ridicule. One entrepreneurial internet user even remixed the senator's speech into a three-minute techno music video that was posted on YouTube. On *The Daily Show,* Jon Stewart joked that Stevens's "series of tubes" comment "sounded like something you'd hear from, let's say, a crazy old man in an airport bar at 3am [rather] than the Chairman of the Senate Commerce Committee."[12]

The snarky blog posts, video remixes, memes, and other parodies of Ted Stevens were effective not because they presented a cogent, rational argument in favor of net neutrality but because they foregrounded a visceral truth about American politics: policy is often not decided by those who are the most knowledgeable about an issue but by those who are most willing to serve corporate power (indeed, Verizon and AT&T were the first- and third-largest contributors to Senator Stevens's 2008 reelection campaign, respectively).[13] Senator Stevens's almost cartoonish performance on the Senate floor, coupled with the satirical depictions of it circulating on the internet, wiped out any pretensions to the contrary. As Peter Dahlgren argues, this kind of humorous commentary works to "strip away artifice, highlight inconsistencies, and generally challenge the authority of official political discourse."[14]

Collaboration of the Titans

Ultimately, none of the net neutrality legislation that was introduced in 2006 was passed into law. However, this initial wave of activism lifted net neutrality from a place of relative obscurity into the national spotlight. Politicians were quickly forced to take a public stance on the issue. During the height of net neutrality activism in 2006, then senator Obama announced his support for net neutrality on a podcast: "We can't have a situation in which the corporate duopoly dictates the future of the Internet, and that's why I'm supporting what is called net neutrality."[15] During his presidential campaign the following year, Obama told a crowd at Google, "I will take a backseat to no one in my commitment to network neutrality."[16]

Barack Obama took office in 2009 with a strong public mandate to implement net neutrality. Yet this early momentum was largely squandered by the Obama administration, which failed to translate the president's ambitious campaign rhetoric into strong net neutrality policy. The new chairman of the Federal Communications Commission, Julius Genachowski, approached the issue with caution. Rather than simply pass net neutrality regulations over the objections of internet service providers, in

June 2010 Genachowski attempted to broker a closed-door agreement between large internet companies and ISPs that would be amenable to each of the stakeholders. The process collapsed in early August 2010 when Google and Verizon—former arch-enemies on the issue of net neutrality, ostensibly representing the two sides of the debate—bypassed the FCC and announced that they had privately arrived at a "legislative framework" for proceeding forward with net neutrality. The Google-Verizon proposal was riddled with loopholes, stripped the FCC of much of its regulatory authority over the wired broadband industry, and conveniently excused wireless internet providers from having to abide by net neutrality.

The Google-Verizon pact was a paradigmatic example of corporate libertarianism, with two of the nation's largest tech behemoths telling the FCC how they would like to be regulated. The joint proposal granted Verizon and other wireless providers the right to throttle their users' internet traffic as long as they were transparent about it. Google, on the other hand, also stood to benefit from the arrangement. Google was trying to make its then little-known mobile operating system, Android, a major player in the mobile world. The year before, Google had reached an agreement with Verizon to run the Android operating system on Verizon's smartphones. The 2010 agreement aimed not only to cement Google's budding partnership with Verizon but to earn goodwill from other wireless carriers in hopes of expanding

Android's footprint. Although the Google-Verizon treaty held no de jure significance, it nevertheless became the cornerstone of the FCC's 2010 Open Internet Order. As a result of Google and Verizon's joint lobbying efforts, wireless carriers were largely exempted from the order.

The reaction to the announcement of the agreement by Google's erstwhile allies in the Save the Internet coalition was swift and severe. The coalition quickly issued a joint press release rebuking the accord: "The Google-Verizon pact isn't just as bad as we feared—it's much worse. They are attacking the internet while claiming to preserve it. Google users won't be fooled."[17] As British Petroleum's Deepwater Horizon oil rig was leaking millions of gallons of crude into the Gulf of Mexico, Free Press senior adviser Marvin Ammori remarked, "You have to hand it to Google. Going from 'Don't Be Evil' to 'Greedier than BP' overnight is a pretty impressive trick."[18]

Mobilizing with less than twenty-four hours' notice, on August 13 protestors peacefully descended upon Google's corporate headquarters in Mountain View, California. James Rucker, the co-founder of the civil rights organization Color of Change, entered Google's building to deliver a petition signed by three hundred thousand people condemning the company's about-face on net neutrality. Outside the GooglePlex, protestors held signs reading, "Google is evil if the price is right" and "No payola for the internet." The Raging Grannies—an activist group com-

Members of the group Raging Grannies protesting outside of Google's corporate headquarters in Mountain View, California. (Photo courtesy of Steve Rhodes.)

prising grandmothers who stage theatrical demonstrations at protest events—even led the crowd in singing "A Battle Hymn for the Internet."

The 2010 Google-Verizon pact revealed the fragility and contradictions at the heart of the Save the Internet coalition. In contrast to most of the public interest groups and activists who supported net neutrality, Google's commitment to protecting net neutrality was fleeting and transactional rather than one of principle. Since its inception, Google has proselytized about the virtues of the open internet in almost romantic terms. For example, in 2005 Google co-founder Sergey Brin waxed poetic: "Technology is an inherent democratizer. Because of the evolution of hardware and software, you're able to scale up almost anything. It means that in our lifetime everyone may have tools of equal power."[19] However, lurking behind Google's soaring rhetoric was always a business model. Net neutrality was essential to the company's early success: without it, in the late 1990s ISPs could have crippled Google in its infancy by blocking or slow-laning traffic to its website or by cutting deals with larger, more established search engines like Yahoo! or MSN to prioritize their traffic.

By 2010, however, it was Google that was the entrenched incumbent. On the one hand, net neutrality protected Google from having to pay ISPs not to throttle its traffic. On the other hand, as Google became one of the largest and most profitable companies in Silicon Valley, it could afford to pay this extortion money; smaller companies looking to compete for Google's market share would be less likely to be able to. Thus, repealing net neutrality would have cut into Google's short-term profits, but potentially cemented its medium- and long-term dominance in search and other markets. As Google's economic interest in net neutrality became more ambiguous, so too did its position on the issue.

2014: Technical Difficulties

After the DC Circuit Court struck down major provisions of the
deeply flawed 2010 Open Internet Order in 2014, Tom Wheeler
spent much of his first year as FCC chairman darting back and
forth between the cable industry, internet companies, and the
occasional public interest group in an ill-fated effort to triangu-
late his way to a solution that would be acceptable to everybody
involved. Wheeler's initial instinct was to strike a compromise
with the broadband cartel, and he was hesitant to acknowledge
what everybody else at the time knew (including the two other
Democratic commissioners who served with him at the FCC):
that the internet is a public utility, and that it ought to be regulated like one.

Frustrated by Tom Wheeler's dithering approach, net neutrality activists put pressure on the FCC to reclassify broadband
internet as a Title II telecommunications service. This was an
ambitious goal at the time, in part because the FCC is a regulatory agency that is generally not as responsive to public pressure
as members of Congress, who face reelection every two years.
Even many activists fighting to reclassify broadband internet
quietly believed that the FCC was unlikely to undertake such a
bold move. Evan Greer, campaign director for the digital rights
group Fight for the Future, reflected that in early 2014, "nobody
thought these Title II net neutrality rules were a remote possibility. . . . I even sat across from an FCC commissioner who told

me outright that it was never going to happen in this political environment."[20]

The grassroots fight for net neutrality in 2014 and 2015 was led by Battle for the Net, a coalition of media advocacy groups. Three major organizations—Free Press, Demand Progress, and Fight for the Future—provided the coalition's staff and funding.[21] Other key participating groups were the Electronic Frontier Foundation, Avaaz, Public Knowledge, the American Civil Liberties Union, Center for Media Justice, Color of Change, the National Hispanic Media Coalition, and Common Cause, among many others.[22] The role of corporations in the Battle for the Net coalition was far less significant in this iteration of the net neutrality saga than it was in 2010. Most notably, many of the Silicon Valley companies that had played a vocal, public-facing role in earlier net neutrality battles were incommunicado on the issue for most of 2014 (the exception being a somewhat perfunctory letter in support of net neutrality that was signed by some of the giants after they were shamed into doing so). Google CEO Eric Schmidt even went so far as to privately chastise members of the Obama administration for embracing Title II reclassification in 2015.[23] As Google, Facebook, and eBay for the most part remained on the sidelines, Netflix became the new corporate face of net neutrality. Netflix was incited to action after Comcast and Verizon throttled Netflix video streaming in late 2013 and early 2014 (Netflix eventually agreed to pay off Comcast, Verizon, and most other major ISPs). Among the other companies that participated in the Battle for the Net actions in 2014 were Etsy, Kickstarter, and OkCupid.

Like the Save the Internet coalition, the Battle for the Net coalition mobilized a populist logic that positioned internet users against the greed of internet service providers. The Battle for the Net website described the fight for net neutrality in this way: "They are Team Cable . . . the most hated companies in America. . . . If they win, the Internet dies. . . . We are Team Internet. . . . We believe in the free and open Internet."[24]

One of the most important ways that net neutrality activists were able to exert pressure on the policymaking process was by encouraging supporters to submit comments about Tom Wheeler's net neutrality proposal to the FCC. The FCC's old, labyrinthine website makes commenting on an issue a cumbersome endeavor even for many technologically savvy internet users. Battle for the Net, the Electronic Frontier Foundation, and other organizations built much more user-friendly interfaces that could be used to submit comments to the FCC. Through email and social media, pro–net neutrality organizations encouraged their members to submit comments. By the end of the FCC's comment deadline in September, over 3.7 million comments had been submitted. According to a study conducted by the Sunlight Foundation, less than 1 percent of the public comments that were submitted to the FCC during the four-month

open-comment period supported Commissioner Wheeler's plan
to divide internet traffic into two speed tiers.[25]

In an effort to illustrate the potential consequences of Tom
Wheeler's plan to allow fast lanes on the internet, the Battle for
the Net coalition coordinated a series of protests dubbed Internet Slowdown Day. The organizers of the protest recruited websites to display the "spinning wheel of death" on their sites on
September 10 in order to re-create the frustrating experience
of waiting for websites to load and "remind everyone what an
Internet without net neutrality would look like." Over forty
thousand websites participated in the protests, including Twitter,
Netflix, Reddit, Tumblr, and Etsy.[26] Visitors to these websites
were prompted to contact their lawmakers to oppose the FCC's
proposal. Internet Slowdown Day generated more than 300,000
calls and 2 million emails to Congress, as well as an additional
777,000 comments to the FCC on September 10 alone.[27]

The Battle for the Net coalition was periodically able to translate its significant online presence into offline action as well.
Throughout 2014, "Team Internet" organized on-the-ground
protests in dozens of cities around the country. Drawing inspi-
ration from the 2011 Occupy Wall Street protests, a small band
of activists called Occupy the FCC set up an encampment outside FCC headquarters in Washington, DC, where they lived and
protested for net neutrality for over a week. Many of these protests took direct aim at FCC commissioner Tom Wheeler. On

The *Nation*'s home page on Internet Slowdown Day, September 10, 2014. (The Nation Magazine, www.thenation.com, September 10, 2014.)

the morning of November 10, demonstrators affiliated with the group Popular Resistance showed up at Tom Wheeler's home and blocked his driveway. "We can't let you go to work today because you work for Comcast, Verizon, and AT&T and not for the people," one protestor told the noticeably agitated FCC chairman. The protestors then broke out into an updated rendition of the famous 1930s union song "Which Side Are You On?" "Which side are you on, Tom? Which side are you on? Are you with the people, Tom, or with the telecoms?"[28]

Despite the yeoman's work performed by net neutrality activists throughout 2014, the most iconic moment of that year's battle came from a comedian. On the June 1, 2014, episode of the HBO show *Last Week Tonight*, John Oliver opened by delivering a thirteen-minute diatribe about net neutrality that would reverberate throughout the internet over the coming weeks and months. Oliver's defense of net neutrality departed from utopian visions of the internet as a Republic of Letters or an ennobled twenty-first-century public sphere, instead embracing a much more quotidian, even hedonistic understanding of the internet as a space of pleasure, rage, and indulgence: "Good evening, monsters. This may be the moment you've spent your whole lives training for . . . for once in your life, we need you to channel that anger, that badly spelled bile that you normally reserve for unforgivable attacks on actresses you seem to think have put on weight, or politicians that you disagree with, or photos of your ex-girlfriend getting on with her life. . . . We need you to get out there and, for once in your life, focus your indiscriminate rage in a useful direction. Seize your moment, my lovely trolls, turn on caps lock, and fly my pretties! Fly! Fly!"[29]

On YouTube alone, John Oliver's video was viewed over 7 million times by January 2015, with the number of "likes" outnumbering the number of "dislikes" by a ratio of one hundred to one.[30] Tom Wheeler himself saw the video and was visibly irritated by John Oliver's jabs at his lobbying past. When asked about Oliver's segment at a press conference, Wheeler shot back, "I am not a dingo," referring to Oliver's quip: "The guy who used to run the cable industry's lobbying arm, is now running the agency tasked with regulating it. That is the equivalent of needing a babysitter and hiring a dingo."[31]

Activist groups including Free Press emailed the Oliver clip to hundreds of thousands of people, further amplifying its reach. Thousands of people who watched John Oliver's net neutrality rant also followed through on his call to flood the FCC's website with comments. The FCC received 3,076 comments in the week before John Oliver's net neutrality sketch aired—the week after, there were 79,838.[32] The barrage of comments crippled the FCC's aging online comment system, which was built on the assumption that only a small number of people—particularly lawyers representing industry groups, local government officials, and the occasional representative of a public interest organization—would be motivated enough to submit comments. The day after Oliver's segment aired, the FCC's website crashed. The FCC's Twitter account announced: "We've been experiencing technical difficulties with our comment system due to heavy traffic. We're working to resolve these issues quickly."[33]

Without the mass public pressure that was brought to bear on him, it is unlikely that Tom Wheeler would have taken the bold step to reclassify broadband internet as a Title II telecommunications service. During his tenure as FCC chairman, Wheeler usually seemed hesitant to implement aggressive reforms, often deferring to the status quo. In the dominant narrative of the 2014 net neutrality battle, Chairman Wheeler's decision to embrace Title II reclassification was a response to pressure from above. On November 10, 2014, days after significant midterm losses for the Democratic Party, President Obama circumvented the FCC and announced his support for strong net neutrality rules directly to the people via YouTube: "I'm urging the Federal Communications Commission to do everything they can to protect net neutrality for everyone. They should make it clear that whether you use a computer, phone, or tablet, internet providers have a legal obligation not to block or limit your access to a website."[34] While some observers decried the move as too little and too late, it was nonetheless a dramatic intervention by the president, and it arguably removed any remaining political cover for Wheeler to pass anything less than a strong net neutrality rule based on Title II protections.

While Obama's "FDR moment" is sometimes pinpointed as the decisive turning point in the net neutrality fight, this assumption does not fully account for the political dynamics at play.[35] Prior to the 2014 wave of activism, President Obama's own support for net neutrality had waned. It was, after all, Obama who had appointed Tom Wheeler as chairman of the FCC the previous year, passing over outspoken consumer advocates such as Harvard Law School professor Susan Crawford, who was the preferred choice of many open internet activists. Obama even

boasted that Wheeler "is the only member of both the cable
television and wireless industry hall of fame. So he is like the
Jim Brown of telecom." Wheeler himself has suggested that his
reversal was the result of his own hard thinking on the matter—
a kind of "road to Damascus" conversion.

Ultimately, however, it was the uproar generated by activists
and ordinary internet users over Chairman Wheeler's proposal
that was critical in securing net neutrality. While Wheeler cer-
tainly deserves credit for his willingness to change course and
enthusiastically defend his position—referring to the passage of
the 2015 Open Internet Order as the "proudest day in his public
policy life"—he acted only after activists paved the way. Notwith-
standing the behind-the-scenes maneuvering that prompted
President Obama to come out so publicly, the strong net neutrality protections passed in 2015 were not simply the result of
an inside game or conflicts among elites. More than anything,
it was a battle fought for and won at the grassroots.

Net Neutrality in the Age of Trump

In recent history, few policies have enjoyed greater support than
net neutrality. On December 12, 2017, the Program for Public
Consultation at the University of Maryland released a poll showing that a large majority of Americans wanted to keep net neutrality rules in place. According to the poll, 83 percent of the
respondents opposed repealing net neutrality, including 75

percent of the Republicans who were surveyed, 89 percent of Democrats, and 86 percent of independents.[36] Two days later, the FCC voted to repeal net neutrality in a 3–2 party-line decision. That such a popular piece of legislation would be repealed under the aegis of a "populist" president who ran on a pledge to "drain the swamp" is something of a tragicomedy. Indeed, Donald Trump's approach to internet and telecommunications policy is thus far largely indistinguishable from the Republican old guard.

With the election of Donald Trump to the presidency on November 8, 2016, the fate of the FCC's 2015 Open Internet Order was immediately imperiled. In a last-ditch effort to preserve net neutrality, a familiar coalition of advocacy organizations—including Fight for the Future, Free Press, Demand Progress, and the Center for Media Justice—coordinated the Internet-Wide Day of Action to Save Net Neutrality on July 12, 2017. The coalition employed many of the same tactics that participants used during the Internet Slowdown Day in 2014, including temporarily changing their websites to simulate what the internet could look like without net neutrality. For example, internet users who visited Reddit on the Day of Action were greeted with a message typed in a crawling speed that read: "The internet's less fun when your favorite sites load slowly, isn't it?" On the top left-hand corner of the website, Redditors inserted the mildly dystopian warning: "Monthly Bandwidth Exceeded, Click to Upgrade."[37]

Meanwhile, Chairman Pai took to the internet for some activism of his own. Dressed in a Santa suit and wielding a lightsaber, he starred in a bizarre video produced by the conservative news site *The Daily Caller* entitled *7 Things You Can Still Do on the Internet After Net Neutrality*. The video stunt was met with immediate contempt by the digital public. On Twitter, the actor who played Luke Skywalker in the *Star Wars* film series, Mark Hamill, cracked that Pai was "profoundly unworthy [to] wield a lightsaber" because "a Jedi acts selflessly for the common man— NOT lie [to] enrich giant corporations."[38] Pai's streak of bad publicity worsened when it was revealed that he had collaborated on the video with a producer named Martina Markota, best known at the time for having helped propagate "Pizzagate," a conspiracy theory that Hillary Clinton and other high-ranking Democratic officials were operating a child-trafficking ring out of the basement of a dingy Washington, DC, pizzeria.[39]

Many of the large tech companies that were at the helm of previous actions to defend net neutrality distanced themselves from the 2017 protests. Google's participation was limited to a short, poorly publicized blog post on its policy blog. Facebook's advocacy consisted of posts by CEO Mark Zuckerberg and Chief Operating Officer Sheryl Sandberg on their personal Facebook pages. Even Netflix, which just three years before had positioned itself as a stalwart defender of net neutrality, made it known that its commitment to net neutrality was largely

FCC chairman Ajit Pai dressed in a Santa Claus costume holding a fidget spinner and toy gun in *The Daily Caller*'s video *7 Things You Can Still Do on the Internet After Net Neutrality.* (*The Daily Caller.*)

circumstantial. Netflix CEO Reed Hastings explained in May 2017, "We think net neutrality is incredibly important," but it is "not narrowly important to us because we're big enough to get the deals we want."[40]

Despite lackluster support from erstwhile corporate allies, net neutrality supporters are continuing the fight on a number of fronts, including in the courts. The major court case, *Mozilla v. FCC*, was brought before the DC Circuit Court of Appeals on February 1, 2019, by media reform organizations, internet companies including Mozilla and Etsy, and the attorney generals of twenty-two states and the District of Columbia. One argument they are making is that the FCC's decision to throw out net neutrality violated the 1946 Administrative Procedure Act, which bans federal agencies from making "arbitrary and capricious" policy changes.[41] Net neutrality advocates contend that the FCC's decision to repeal the 2015 Open Internet Order just three years after it was passed was based not on a careful assessment of the effectiveness of the law but on the ideological whims of the FCC's newly minted Republican majority.

In the spring of 2018, Senator Ed Markey spearheaded a Hail Mary effort in the Senate to prevent the repeal of net neutrality from going into effect through the Congressional Review Act, which allows Congress to reverse recent decisions by government agencies with a simple majority in the House and Senate coupled with the president's approval. Although the measure passed 52–47 in the Senate—a remarkable feat considering that Republicans controlled the chamber—it failed to garner a majority of support in the Republican-controlled House. After the 2018 midterm elections, Democrats took back the House, bolstering the number of pro–net neutrality members of Congress. Nonetheless, President Trump would likely veto such a resolution if it were to reach his desk.

Absent action to reinstitute net neutrality at the federal level, activists have engaged in a state-by-state fight to reimplement net neutrality. As of February 2019, ten states have enacted net neutrality legislation, while more than twenty others are considering it. On September 30, 2018, California passed a net neutrality bill that the Electronic Frontier Foundation called the "gold standard" of state net neutrality laws. In fact, California's bill goes even further than the FCC's 2015 Open Internet Order.[42] In addition to restoring rules against blocking, throttling, and paid prioritization, California's bill also forbids ISPs from engaging in a controversial practice called zero-rating, which was permitted under the previous net neutrality rules. Zero-rating allows ISPs to exempt certain websites or applications from counting toward users' data charges. This gives ISPs the power to make it easier and cheaper to access websites they favor and more expensive to access those they disfavor.

If California's net neutrality bill is successfully implemented, its impact could reverberate across the country. Enacting strong net neutrality regulations in the country's most populous state could push broadband providers to abide by net neutrality principles even in states with weak or nonexistent net neutrality laws. Rather than adopting a different approach to net neutrality in every state they operate in—a costly, logistically complicated, and technically complex endeavor—internet service providers may be pressured into bringing their traffic management practices into line with California's standards.

These state-led efforts to protect net neutrality have been met with fierce opposition from the FCC, President Trump's Department of Justice, and the broadband industry, which all insist that these rules are illegal. Yet their argument rests on shaky grounds. In voting to repeal net neutrality in December 2017, the FCC's Republican commissioners claimed that the agency lacked the authority to enact federal-level net neutrality regulation. At the same time, the FCC is asserting sweeping authority to preempt state and local governments from creating their own net neutrality rules. The FCC cannot have it both ways. As Stanford Law professor Barbara van Schewick explains, "An agency that has no power to regulate has no power to preempt the states, according to case law."[43] Gigi Sohn adds: "The broadband providers say they don't want state laws, they want federal laws. But they were the driving force behind the federal rules being repealed."[44]

Indeed, the opposition to these state-led initiatives reeks of cynical political opportunism: for decades, Republicans have extolled the virtue of states' rights and decried the excessive influence of the federal government on local affairs. ISPs and their political surrogates have also long mobilized states' rights arguments in defense of the broadband industry's interests, whether in opposition to federal net neutrality laws or in support of state bills prohibiting municipalities from building their own broadband networks to compete with large ISPs. Now, faced with a wave of state-led movements to protect net neutrality, ISPs insist that the fate of net neutrality should be decided by Congress rather than by state legislatures.

Their Net Neutrality and Ours

For the likes of Google, Netflix, and Facebook, the value of net neutrality is expressed almost exclusively in commercial terms. A 2017 report published by the Internet Association, the lobbying arm for companies such as Google, Amazon, and Facebook, summarized the net neutrality debate as follows: "Behind all the noise surrounding net neutrality, the debate boils down to . . . competition, investment, capacity, and innovation."[45] In this view, net neutrality is first and foremost a series of principles to encourage innovation and entrepreneurship on the internet. The public interest is either of secondary concern or—perhaps even more problematically—equated with the health of digital capitalism itself.

During earlier stages of the net neutrality debate, activists sometimes failed to distinguish their own political goals from those of Google, Netflix, and other fair-weather corporate crusaders for net neutrality. Too often they took on the pro-business arguments of their corporate counterparts, substituting rationales for net neutrality based on civil rights, free speech, and social justice for ones based on promoting innovation and entrepreneurship. There was a tendency to equate the public's interest in net neutrality with the success of Google, Facebook, or the "next" new media titan, effectively entrusting the public good to private enterprise.

However, many activists no longer want to be coalition partners with Silicon Valley tech giants. Over the last decade, the likes of Facebook and Google have not just been fickle allies in the fight for net neutrality, they have also actively worked to undermine the open internet. There is growing public recognition that Facebook and Google are not neutral conduits of interpersonal communication and information exchange but rapacious corporations that are intent on monetizing their users' privacy for commercial gain. Facebook and Google have helped transform the internet from what idealists in the first decade of the twenty-first century hoped would be a democratic public sphere into a commercialized panopticon littered with advertisements, clickbait, and misinformation. A broad-based movement for net neutrality therefore requires a much stronger ethical foundation than the business interests of Facebook, Google, and Amazon. At the forefront of the current wave of net neutrality activism are groups like the Center for Media Justice and Color of Change, which have reframed net neutrality as a civil rights and social justice issue rather than as an internecine quarrel between different segments of corporate America. Malkia Cyril, the executive director of the Center for Media Justice, explains, "This is not a fight between Comcast and Netflix. This is not a fight between the geeks and the nerds. This is a fight between ordinary people and our right to access a modern communications system in the twenty-first century and those who would like to discriminate and use that system for profit instead of for democracy."[46]

Fundamentally, the fight for net neutrality is a fight for political power. In the age of Trump, net neutrality is of particular importance to the emerging democratic movements that are fighting on the front lines against the rising forces of racism, nativism, sexism, and economic exploitation that have been empowered by the Far Right. From Black Lives Matter to the #MeToo movement to the Dakota Access Pipeline protests (#NODAPL), digital tools, including social media platforms, offer activists an imperfect but efficient means to broadcast their message to the public. The utility of the internet to marginalized communities is, in part, dependent on net neutrality. As the media justice activist Steven Renderos argues: "In an era when immigrant and Muslim communities are being scapegoated by the White House, an open Internet protected by Title II is vital to preserving our democracy. When the Muslim Ban was announced, activists used the open Internet to mobilize millions at airports across the country."[47]

CONCLUSION

On the eve of the Great Depression, just three holding companies generated nearly half of the electricity in the United States.[1] These largely unregulated companies offered electricity to big cities and wealthy customers at inflated prices while passing over large swaths of the country that were deemed insufficiently profitable for them to service. Although considered a novel luxury at the turn of the century, by the 1920s electricity was an essential part of participating in modern economic and political life. Franklin Delano Roosevelt made public power a central plank of his successful 1932 presidential campaign, asserting that private utilities had "selfish purposes" and that "never shall the federal government part with its sovereignty or with its control of its power resources while I'm president of the United States."[2] Roosevelt followed through on his promise. Once elected, he established the Tennessee Valley Authority, a federally owned utility tasked with bringing affordable electricity to seven states in the rural South. What we are seeing today with broadband internet is in many ways reminiscent of the 1930s. What we need is a New Deal for the digital age.

At a time in which even modest protections that prevent corporations from usurping the public interest are being jettisoned, we must dare to think boldly about the future of our broadband infrastructure. The time for tinkering is over. Net neutrality is a necessary but insufficient policy for creating a more democratic internet. It is designed to curb the abuses of large internet service providers, but it does not fundamentally challenge their market power. Nor does it directly confront ongoing inequalities in internet access. If we are to rescue the internet's democratic potential from the grip of the broadband cartel, net neutrality must be one part of a much more ambitious political program.

So what (else) is to be done? What policies are capable of reining in corporate control of the internet and opening up public access to this critical infrastructure? We need a more comprehensive policy plan for a democratic internet. While some of this policy agenda may seem ambitious, we take heart in the vibrant activism in support of net neutrality in recent years as well as in the public's growing concern over Facebook's and Google's business practices. Indeed, the public's engagement with media and communication policy issues is unprecedented. A fertile opportunity to democratize the internet has opened before us. We must not squander it.

Policy Interventions for Democratizing the Internet

Net neutrality addresses a problem that lies downstream from a more fundamental issue: the political and economic power of the broadband cartel. A more democratic internet is possible, but only if we confront the monopoly power of ISPs. There are three general strategies for bringing them to heel: breaking up the broadband cartel, imposing strict public interest obligations on them, and building publicly owned alternatives.[3] These three strategies need not be pursued in isolation of one another—each can form a part of a multipronged assault on the broadband cartel's control over the nation's internet infrastructure.

The first approach to weakening the grip of the broadband cartel over our digital infrastructure is the anti-monopoly option. In recent years, a fast-growing anti-monopoly movement in the United States has offered a piercing critique of the extreme and growing concentration in most sectors of the American economy.[4] In the context of broadband internet markets, the anti-monopoly option prescribes resuscitating long-dormant anti-trust legislation in order to break up (horizontally and vertically) large ISPs such as Comcast into smaller units—or at least prevent them from accruing even more economic power than they already have by blocking future mergers and acquisitions. The objective is to create a much more decentralized and competitive economic environment in which numerous small and medium-sized ISPs vigorously compete for customers on the basis of price, speed, and quality of service.

While it is an essential tool to have at our disposal to discipline or prevent monopolies, one limitation of the antitrust approach is that it can fail to adequately address commercial excesses in America's communication systems. The ire of anti-monopoly activists is often directed more at the lack of competition that ISPs face and less toward the commercial values underpinning corporate power. In this approach, critical questions about how the internet should be governed are still largely delegated to the market.

A second approach is to impose strict public interest regulations on ISPs.[5] Monopolies—especially natural monopolies—are typically obliged to abide by a social contract in which they are required to provide for critical social needs in exchange for the right to operate at scale. Telephone and cable firms have gradually been allowed to shed these responsibilities to the public as a result of the liberalization of the telecommunications industry over the last three decades. Yet it is important to remember that ISPs are not granting us access to some private luxury; they are instead merely temporary managers of a critical infrastructure that provides a public service we all require. We as a society grant them the privilege to profit from this public good, but only if they continue to serve us accordingly. In many ways, net neutrality protections fall within this category of public interest regulation. A long history of policy battles demonstrates that communication monopolies have been very successful in weakening these regulations over time.

The third strategy is to create truly public alternatives to corporate internet service providers. Although opponents of municipal broadband like Republican FCC commissioner Michael O'Rielly frame these initiatives as inimical to the American free market tradition—calling it "a perverse form of socialism"—there is also a long history in America of managing essential utilities such as water, sewage, and electricity at the municipal level.[6] As we saw in chapter 1, previous generations of Americans advocated for municipalizing and nationalizing telecommunication services. Similarly, Franklin Delano Roosevelt argued that "where a community . . . is not satisfied with the service rendered or the rates charged by the private utility, it has the undeniable basic right . . . to set up, after a fair referendum to its voters has been had, its own governmentally owned and operated service." Roosevelt characterized this right as "a 'birch rod' in the cupboard to be taken out and used only when the 'child' gets beyond the point where a mere scolding does no good."[7]

Compared with most other leading democracies, the United States is weak in all three areas discussed above: breaking up monopolies, regulating monopolies, and creating public alternatives. Nonetheless, this last approach offers, in our view, the best chance to circumvent the stranglehold of corporate monopolies over last-mile access to the internet. The "public option" is worth closer attention.

Beyond the "Birch Rod": The Public Options

Following Roosevelt's quite violent metaphor, public ownership of internet infrastructure should be seen as more than a "birch rod"—an internet service provider of last resort that is used to discipline out-of-control ISPs into offering more competitive pricing, upgrading their infrastructure, or expanding their service area. In fact, publicly owned and managed internet service is more than a threat to the broadband cartel: it can be a viable alternative to it. Removing the internet from the commercial market is the most surefire way of guaranteeing that the public interest is privileged above corporate profits. Indeed, this is traditionally how public goods—such as education—are treated in democratic societies. These services are too precious to leave entirely to the market.

The internet can be delivered like other publicly owned services. In recent years, many cities and towns across the country have taken it upon themselves to build their own municipal broadband networks. When not felled by the plague of austerity, motivated municipalities are often more capable of mustering the capital needed to construct a next-generation broadband network than independent ISPs. Today, more than 750 communities in the United States offer publicly owned cable or fiber to the home (FTTH) broadband networks. FTTH networks provide much higher download and upload speeds than internet provided over coaxial or copper telephone wires, traveling at about 70 percent of the speed of light.[8]

Frustrated with the unwillingness of Comcast and AT&T to upgrade their dilapidated infrastructure or to expand their service to less profitable neighborhoods, the city of Chattanooga, Tennessee, took the bold step of constructing a FTTH network in 2009. The city operates the network through its electrical company, which offers customers a one gigabyte per second internet connection and television service for $70 a month. By almost any measure, Chattanooga's experiment has been an unmitigated success: according to a 2018 survey conducted by *Consumer Reports*, Chattanooga's municipal broadband network is the top-rated internet service provider operating in the country.[9] Similar municipal broadband initiatives in places like Santa Monica, California, and Sandy, Oregon, have also been immensely successful. In general, community-owned FTTH networks are cheaper, faster, and more transparent than their private sector counterparts, despite the fact that they lack the gigantic economies of scale that broadband behemoths like Comcast and Verizon enjoy.[10]

In terms of market share, the threat posed to monopoly ISPs by municipal broadband is still quite modest: there are relatively few publicly owned wired broadband networks, and they tend to be confined to small and medium-sized markets. Yet the broadband cartel has been fighting an aggressive campaign to limit municipal broadband expansion for more than a decade. In Fort Collins, Colorado, which has a population of 161,000, Comcast poured almost $1 million into a campaign to dissuade voters from endorsing a municipal broadband initiative.[11] Under intense lobbying pressure by the broadband cartel and its trade groups, twenty-six states have implemented laws that severely restrict or prohibit municipalities from building their own broadband network.[12]

What the broadband cartel fears, then, is less the near-term loss of market share than the long-term threat of a good example. America's internet service providers are consistently ranked among the most loathed companies in the country. By contrast, recent polling suggests that municipal broadband initiatives, or at least the right to undertake them, enjoy overwhelming bipartisan support among the public. Seven in ten Americans believe that local governments should have the right to build their own high-speed internet networks, including 67 percent of Republicans and 74 percent of Democrats.[13] The success of publicly owned broadband initiatives shows that a communication system dominated by the likes of Comcast and Verizon is neither inevitable nor necessary. Municipal broadband prefigures what an alternative communications system—one committed to maximizing the public good rather than corporate profits—might look like.

A number of public broadband projects have also been proposed at the state level. In May 2018, Michigan gubernatorial candidate Abdul El-Sayed laid out a statewide public option for internet service called MI-Fi. El-Sayed's plan involved forging "public-public" partnerships in which the state would work closely with cities and municipalities to finance and construct publicly owned fiber internet networks.[14] Vermont gubernatorial candidate Christine Hallquist also proposed building a publicly owned statewide fiber internet network.[15] Although these candidates did not win their respective elections, their policy proposals are worth further consideration.

Pursuing broadband development at the state rather than at the municipal level offers a number of substantial advantages. Municipal broadband initiatives are by their very nature highly localized, fragmented projects. They require that individual communities levy massive amounts of political capital, technical expertise, and legal resources to create and maintain them. Many municipalities, particularly low-income ones that have a small tax base, simply do not have these resources at their disposal. By contrast, statewide broadband initiatives would benefit from much larger economies of scale than municipal-level initiatives, spreading the costs of building out and maintaining the network over a much larger number of people.

Ultimately, the most desirable path forward may be a federal-level "Fiber for All" program. Only a Fiber for All plan could offer a high-speed, neutral internet that is truly universal in scope and could serve Americans regardless of what city, state, or zip code they live in. While this proposal would likely encounter immense political resistance from the broadband cartel, progressive politicians and even many activists seem to underestimate the public's appetite for a bold solution to the decrepit state of America's privately owned and operated internet infrastructure. According to a 2018 poll administered by Data for Progress, 56 percent of Americans support a public option for the internet, compared to just 28 percent who oppose it.[16]

Politically, guaranteeing affordable and reliable broadband access to all members of the public is a compelling position for either major political party in the United States to adopt. A Fiber for All plan specifically appeals to the material interests of rural voters who are underserved by the cable and telecom giants but wield significant influence over American elections.[17] Regardless of the political benefits attached to supporting broadband internet expansion, the existence of "internet deserts"—whether in rural areas or in poor urban neighborhoods—is simply unacceptable in an immensely wealthy democratic nation such as the U.S. Confronting this injustice will require a broad-based grassroots struggle.

Despite the benefits of a Fiber for All plan, there are concerns that public ownership of internet infrastructure, whether at the municipal, state, or federal level, will increase the threat of government surveillance.[18] Several important measures must be taken to preempt this possibility. First and foremost, a strong, independent government agency should be chartered to build and administer the network. In addition, any municipal, state, or federal government agency that operates a public broadband network should be required to abide by the following principles:

- Any web browsing, device, or location data beyond what is absolutely necessary to maintain the technical performance of the broadband network will not be collected.
- Any user data that is collected for the purposes of network management will be immediately anonymized.
- User data will not be shared with law enforcement or any government agency except when legally required by a court warrant. In such instances, users will be notified in a reasonable and timely fashion that their data has been shared.

- User data will not be sold to or otherwise shared with any third parties except, as necessary, with contractors working on building out or improving the network.

- Users will have the right to request a dossier that details all of the personal information that the public ISP has collected, who that information has been shared with, and the purpose for which it has been shared.

- An independent oversight and review board consisting of a wide range of privacy experts and representative members of civil society will be established to periodically review the privacy practices of any public broadband internet operator.

With the proper institutional safeguards in place, we need not choose between providing universal, affordable internet access and preserving the privacy of internet users.

Major Impediments to the "Internet for All" Policy Agenda

Despite the popularity of many of these proposed reforms, to accomplish any of them we must first break through the corporate libertarian policy paradigm, a framework that does not recognize the internet as a critical infrastructure whose democratic purpose far exceeds the commercial imperatives of internet service monopolies. Dismantling this libertarian framework requires undoing its major underpinning—a significant impediment to any progress toward establishing a new policy paradigm and democratizing the internet: regulatory capture.

The FCC is currently a textbook example of "regulatory capture," a situation in which a government agency loses its independence by internalizing the commercial logics and value systems of the very industries that it is supposed to regulate.[19] One major contributing factor to regulatory capture is the revolving door between the FCC and the telecommunications and cable industries. For decades, FCC personnel have left the agency to serve the very industries they previously oversaw; one analysis by the media reform organization Free Press found that of the twenty-seven commissioners and chairs who served on the FCC between 1980 and 2018, at least twenty-three had followed this career path.[20]

The thin line separating regulators from the regulated has all but disappeared. While former FCC commissioner Michael Copps (who remained a media reform activist at Common Cause and the Benton Foundation after he left the FCC, and currently sits on the board of Free Press) is a notable exception, the career trajectory of former FCC chairman Michael Powell demonstrates the rule.[21] For the past seven years, Powell has been president and CEO of the NCTA, the top cable lobbying group, and an outspoken advocate for all manner of pro-telecom policies. Other cases have been even more egregious, such as when former FCC commissioner Meredith Atwell Baker left her post to become a lobbyist for Comcast just four months after voting to approve that company's mega-merger with NBC.[22] Baker now heads the CTIA, the wireless trade association.[23]

The regulatory capture of the FCC by corporate interests—a phenomenon that permeates many other areas of government—over time contributes to a broader ideological and discursive capture.[24] Policy discourse becomes limited to objectives that are aligned with corporate interests, and policymakers systematically write off alternative options like subsidizing public media, enforcing public interest obligations, and trust-busting corporate monopolies and cartels.[25] This discourse infiltrates think tanks, regulatory agencies, and even academic research.[26] Such discursive framing helps justify regulatory retreat—in recent decades often referred to as "deregulation"—which contributes to pervasive and systemic market failures throughout our contemporary media system.

A related development might be described as "digital Lochnerism," which harkens back to the Lochner era of American jurisprudence. In the namesake 1905 case, *Lochner v. New York,* the Supreme Court struck down a state labor law that set the maximum allowable daily and weekly hours for bakers on the basis that it violated the due process clause of the Fourteenth Amendment and the constitutional protection of the "liberty of contract." This period of legal history, which extended from the *Lochner* ruling to the New Deal, saw the courts invalidate approximately two hundred pieces of state and federal legislation, much of which attempted to regulate the behavior of commercial firms by establishing minimum wage protections and banking regulations.[27] Thus, the term *Lochnerization* refers to a kind of judicial activism characterized by economic libertarianism that invalidates regulations according to a perverse reading of the due process clause. This kind of legal thinking, also evident in the infamous *Citizens United* decision, essentially bestows corporations with the constitutional rights of citizens.[28]

The specific ideological threat facing the internet's democratic potential in recent years is what Susan Crawford identifies as "First Amendment Lochnerism," in which the economic interests of large ISPs are protected by a corrupted interpretation of the First Amendment that protects corporate malfeasance.[29] Verizon used a similar line of reasoning during its earlier arguments to the DC Circuit Court, and comparable arguments are currently being advanced in various arenas.[30] While many scoffed at these arguments during earlier net neutrality cases, one person did seem to embrace them: the new Supreme Court justice Brett Kavanaugh. In a 2017 dissenting opinion while he was sitting on the DC Circuit Court, Kavanaugh indicated that he thinks internet access providers should hold "speaker" privileges, stating that "the First Amendment bars the Government from restricting the editorial discretion of Internet service providers."[31]

These corporate libertarian arguments aim to exploit the First Amendment to delegitimize government intervention in the economy and thus render the state powerless to address the deep structural inequities that plague the nation's telecommunications sector. Opposing this ideological framework will require legal and normative rationales for state intervention. At the most general level, such policy rationales should draw from the previously mentioned economic theories of market failure and public goods. These arguments should also be adopted from democratic theories based on positive freedoms that privilege freedom of expression and the affirmative right to access diverse sources of information. Such guarantees go beyond the libertarian definition of freedom as merely the absence of state interference. Frameworks based on market failure and positive freedoms undercut the libertarian foundation for rationalizing a commercialized internet that serves corporate monopoly interests above all others.

Pipe Dreams and Nightmares

Although the recent battles over net neutrality may seem unprecedented, we have faced similar moments before.[32] Throughout the nineteenth and twentieth centuries, the emergence of new media, including the telegraph, radio, and telephone, spawned conflicts over their ownership, governance, and whose interests they should ultimately serve. As we once again set out to answer core questions about how to govern a new medium, we might look to our past to discern lessons for charting our future. The media system that we have today—one that is dominated by a small number of lightly regulated corporations—was neither inevitable nor natural; it was the result of policy battles and the triumph of commercial interests over the public interest.

The country's media infrastructure has undergone periodic confluences of technological, political, and social tumult—what historians sometimes call "critical junctures."[33] Critical junctures are periods in history in which the certainties and commonsense beliefs of previous eras are abruptly thrown into question and new trajectories are made possible. American history is punctuated with these paradigm-shifting moments, which typically originate at the grassroots level and gradually gain expression among progressive political elites. These fleeting moments create rare windows of opportunity for radical ideas to flourish. One such inflection point occurred in the 1940s during policy battles over radio, which resulted in America's preeminent medium being largely captured and degraded by a corporate oligopoly. With the public airwaves marred by excessive advertising and low-quality programming, many felt that extreme commercialism was undermining radio's revolutionary promise. The 1940s witnessed the rise and fall of a media reform movement that attempted to establish a social democratic alternative to the commercial media system. While reformers were able to force the breakup of NBC (the largest radio monopoly) and institute some important public interest policies such as the Fairness Doctrine, this reform movement largely failed. Nonetheless, we can glean important lessons from this past struggle.

We once again occupy an indeterminate point in the history of a new medium. Will the internet fulfill its democratic promise and empower citizens to participate in the public sphere, or will it turn into a soapbox for large corporations and the 1 percent? American history shows that society has suffered under monopolies before—and that citizens have stood up to confront them. And if this history provides any lesson, it is that reforming our media system will require continued public pressure from below, not just from political elites. It also will require removing the intellectual and ideological blinders that prevent our government from taking on media monopolies in a serious structural way. Policy battles from previous eras suggest that media corporations cannot simply be shamed into acting responsibly. They must be compelled to do so, especially from below by social movements.[34]

As these grassroots movements coalesce, an important aim is to democratize *all* areas of the internet. A public option for broadband access is an important first step at challenging the power of internet service monopolies, but we must also confront other digital injustices. Platform monopolies such as Facebook (which also owns Instagram and WhatsApp) and Google (which also owns YouTube) hold tremendous gatekeeping control over internet content and engage in "surveillance capitalism" in the United States and around the world—and their power is only growing.[35] Confronting the full range of "digital feudalism," in which corporate oligopolies capture multiple layers of the internet—including control over content, intellectual property, and technological hardware—will require a multiplicity of movements and activist campaigns to democratize all aspects of the internet.[36] This should also include confronting inequities across the globe: billions of people still lack internet access, and in many countries internet users are subject to surveillance, political propaganda, online hate speech, and other injustices.

Some positive signs suggest that a broad-based movement for a democratic internet is beginning to stir. Calls for revitalizing America's antitrust traditions, as well as a focus on local and state-level policy interventions, are gaining momentum. But challenging the corporate domination of the internet will take long-term organizing and tremendous grassroots energy. It is uncertain whether the same force that advanced net neutrality can be harnessed to confront the structural roots of internet monopolies. The level of engagement, from petitions to public comments to the FCC, shows that business-as-usual—in which policymakers make decisions on the public's behalf without the public's consent—is no longer tenable. This democratic shift alone is grounds for cautious optimism.

One of the slogans from earlier media reform movements is that whatever your first political issue is, media reform should be your second. Oppositional political movements require an open media system in order to win popular support. Without net neutrality, there is a greater likelihood that corporate censorship will deprive movements of the public outreach they need to grow. However, an engaged public can organize to push back against corporate libertarianism and finally establish a medium guided by social justice. How this battle is resolved could determine whether we follow the path of earlier communication infrastructures, whose great potential was squandered in favor of crass commercialism—or whether we can finally begin to create a media system worthy of its democratic promise.

March 14, 2002: Under the leadership of Republican-appointed chairman Michael Powell, the FCC reclassifies internet access provided over cable wires as an "information service."

June 2002: Tim Wu coins the term *network neutrality* in a short policy memo. The following year, Wu expands on this concept in his seminal work "Network Neutrality, Broadband Discrimination," *Journal on Telecommunications and High Technology Law* 2 (2003): 23–68.

October 6, 2003: The Ninth Circuit Court of Appeals rules that cable companies (like Comcast and Time Warner) are required to sell access to their networks to independent ISPs (like Earthlink and Brand X).

June 27, 2005: The Supreme Court decides in favor of ISPs in the case of *National Cable & Telecommunications Association v. Brand X Internet Services*. The ruling effectively ends open access, a policy that forced telephone monopolies to lease their lines to independent ISPs.

February 2007: Robb Topolski, a former software quality engineer at Intel, discovers that Comcast is blocking and throttling traffic to the peer-to-peer file-sharing client BitTorrent.

August 1, 2008: The FCC sanctions Comcast for blocking and throttling traffic to BitTorrent, marking the first time that a broadband provider is reprimanded by the FCC for violating net neutrality.

April 6, 2010: The U.S. Court of Appeals for the D.C. Circuit Court finds that the FCC does not have the regulatory authority to enforce net neutrality.

December 21, 2010: The FCC issues the Open Internet Order preventing ISPs from blocking or slowing down consumer access to content on the internet, but leaving open the possibility that ISPs could create fast lanes for certain content providers.

January 14, 2014: The U.S. Court of Appeals for the D.C. Circuit Court throws out most of the FCC's 2010 Open Internet Order on narrow jurisdictional grounds.

February 26, 2015: Led by Chairman Tom Wheeler, the FCC votes to institute strong net neutrality protections by reclassifying broadband internet as a Title II telecommunications service.

June 14, 2016: The U.S. Court of Appeals for the D.C. Circuit Court upholds the new Open Internet Order.

December 4, 2017: Under the chairmanship of Ajit Pai, the FCC votes to approve the Restoring Internet Freedom Order, which rolls back the net neutrality regulations that were put in place by the FCC in 2015.

INTRODUCTION

1. Jon Brodkin, "Verizon Throttled Fire Department's 'Unlimited' Data during Calif. Wildfire," *Ars Technica*, August 21, 2018, https://arstechnica.com/tech-policy/2018/08/verizon-throttled-fire-departments-unlimited-data-during-calif-wildfire/.

2. Initially, the net neutrality debate was largely confined to academia and industry. Within academia, the most prominent battle was fought between Tim Wu, a vocal proponent of net neutrality and progenitor of the term, and Christopher Yoo, one of the most influential skeptics of net neutrality. See, for example, Tim Wu and Christopher Yoo, "Keeping the Internet Neutral? Tim Wu and

Christopher Yoo Debate," *Federal Communications Law Journal* 59, no. 3 (2007): 575–92.

3. Jerome H. Saltzer, David P. Reed, and David D. Clark, "End-to-End Arguments in System Design," *ACM Transactions on Computer Systems (TOCS)* 2, no. 4 (1984): 277–88.

4. Roxanda Elliott, "How Page Load Time Affects Bounce Rate and Page Views," *Section.Io,* August 10, 2017, https://www.section.io/blog/page-load-time-bounce-rate/. See also Daniel An and Pat Meenan, "Why Marketers Should Care about Mobile Page Speed," *Think with Google,* July 2016, https://www.thinkwithgoogle.com/marketing-resources/experience-design/mobile-page-speed-load-time/.

5. Given that net neutrality has evolved into one of the most contentious public policy debates in the history of American telecommunications, the relative dearth of in-depth book-length studies about the subject is somewhat surprising. Dawn C. Nunziato's book *Virtual Freedom: Net Neutrality and Free Speech in the Internet Age* (Stanford: Stanford University Press, 2009) discusses the manifold threats to free speech online emanating from the private sector, including internet service providers as well as other powerful private conduits of online expression such as Google. Another exception is Zack Stiegler's edited volume *Regulating the Web: Network Neutrality and the Fate of the Open Internet* (Lanham, MD: Lexington Books, 2013), which features the history, politics, and ideologies animating the net neutrality debate. Other key books often associated with the net neutrality debate actually deal only tangentially with the issue but provide critical political and economic context. For example,

Susan Crawford's excellent *Captive Audience: The Telecom Industry and Monopoly Power in the New Gilded Age* (New Haven: Yale University Press, 2004) provides a rigorous history of how today's telecommunications monopolies came into being. Longtime net neutrality advocate Marvin Ammori has written a short e-book on the subject titled *On Internet Freedom* (Elkat Books, 2013). There is also a growing body of scholarship about net neutrality in academic journals, including two special issues devoted to net neutrality in the *International Journal of Communication*, published in 2007 and 2016. For an early article linking net neutrality and the history of common carrier regulations, see Christian Sandvig, "Network Neutrality Is the New Common Carriage," *Info: The Journal of Policy, Regulation, and Strategy* 9, nos. 2–3 (2006): 136–47. For an early article advocating for a bolder policy vision beyond net neutrality, see Sascha Meinrath and Victor Pickard, "The New Network Neutrality: Criteria for Internet Freedom," *International Journal of Communication Law and Policy* 12 (2008): 225–43. For an excellent overview of the history of net neutrality, see Harold Feld, "The History of Net Neutrality in 13 Years of Tales of the Sausage Factory (with a Few Additions)," *WetMachine*, January 10, 2018, https://wetmachine.com/tales-of-the-sausage-factory/the-history-of-net-neutrality-in-13-years-of-tales-of-the-sausage-factory-with-a-few-additions-part-i/.

6. The dominant business-oriented approach to net neutrality is evident both in books that support net neutrality, including Barbara van Schewick's *Internet Architecture and Innovation* (Cambridge, MA: MIT Press, 2012) and Tim Wu's *The Master*

Switch: The Rise and Fall of Information Empires (New York: Knopf, 2011), and works that oppose it, such as Thomas Hazlett's *The Fallacy of Net Neutrality* (New York: Encounter Books, 2011).

7. A great exception to this tendency is the work by media scholar Russell Newman, who carefully situates the net neutrality debate within a much wider historical and political economic context. See Russell Newman, *The Paradoxes of Network Neutralities* (Cambridge, MA: MIT Press, forthcoming).

CHAPTER 1. THE BATTLE FOR OWNERSHIP AND CONTROL OF COMMUNICATION INFRASTRUCTURES

1. These ideological positions are detailed in Victor Pickard, *America's Battle for Media Democracy: The Triumph of Corporate Libertarianism and the Future of Media Reform* (New York: Cambridge University Press, 2015).

2. For an excellent overview of this early history of the internet and its privatization, see Ben Tarnoff, "The Internet Should Be a Public Good," *Jacobin*, August 31, 2016, https://www.jacobin mag.com/2016/08/internet-public-dns-privatization-icann -netflix/. For an authoritative history of the creation of the internet, see Janet Abbate, *Inventing the Internet* (Cambridge, MA: MIT Press, 1999). See also Dan Schiller, *Digital Capitalism: Networking the Global Market System* (Cambridge, MA: MIT Press, 1999).

3. These figures are from Rajiv C. Shah and Jay P. Kesan, "The Privatization of the Internet's Backbone Network," *Journal of Broadcasting & Electronic Media* 51, no. 1 (2007): 93–109.

4. Robert McChesney, "Between Cambridge and Palo Alto," *Catalyst* 2, no. 1 (2018), https://catalyst-journal.com/vol2/no1/between -cambridge-and-palo-alto.

5. Tim Wu, "A Proposal for Network Neutrality," June 2002, http://www.timwu.org/OriginalNNProposal.pdf.

6. For a magisterial history of U.S. postal policy, see Richard R. John, *Spreading the News: The American Postal System from Franklin to Morse* (Cambridge, MA: Harvard University Press, 1995).

7. For authoritative histories of American telecommunications, see Richard R. John, *Network Nation: Inventing American Tele- communications* (Cambridge, MA: Harvard University Press, 2010) and Robert MacDougall, *The People's Network: The Polit- ical Economy of the Telephone in the Gilded Age* (Philadelphia: University of Pennsylvania Press, 2014). MacDougall's book also looks at Canadian telecommunications history. Both books take advantage of an SBC archive based in San Antonio that opened up in the early 2000s. Access to these new materials has shifted the historiography by complicating AT&T-centric historical narratives. For an excellent social history of American telecommunications, see Dan Schiller's forthcoming book *From Post Office to Internet: The Missing History of US Telecommuni- cations*.

8. John, *Network Nation,* 170–99.

9. Paul Starr, *The Creation of the Media* (New York: Basic Books, 2004), 189. Parts of this historical analysis draw from Meinrath and Pickard, "The New Network Neutrality," 225–43. See also Sascha Meinrath and Victor Pickard, "Transcending Net Neu-

trality: Ten Steps toward an Open Internet," *Journal of Internet Law* 12, no. 6 (2008): 1, 12–21.

10. Schiller, *From Post Office to Internet*.

11. MacDougall, *The People's Network*, 94–101. Another important telephone-related popular movement was the public uprising around the rechartering of the Chicago Telephone Company's franchise agreement in 1907. See John, *Network Nation*, 327–39.

12. MacDougall, *The People's Network*, 132–73; Starr, *The Creation of the Media*, 193.

13. Starr, *The Creation of the Media*, 201–2.

14. MacDougall, *The People's Network*, 1–18.

15. John, *Network Nation*, 263–68. See also MacDougall, *The People's Network*, 174, and Schiller, *From Post Office to Internet*.

16. For an excellent treatment of this historical struggle and its outcomes, see John, *Network Nation*, 370–406. Michael A. Janson and Christopher S. Yoo, "The Wires Go to War: The U.S. Experiment with Government Ownership of the Telephone System During World War I" (2013). *Faculty Scholarship*. Paper 467. http://scholarship.law.upenn.edu/faculty_scholarship/467.

17. Richard John points out that the name of the antitrust suit's resolution is more accurately the McReynolds settlement. See *Network Nation*, 359–63.

18. John, *Network Nation*. See also Schiller, *From Post Office to Internet*.

19. Network effects refers to how a network's value grows as its membership increases, thus creating a kind of path dependency that is difficult to reverse as it becomes increasingly irrational for new members to join smaller networks.

20. AT&T held a near monopoly over the domestic telephone service; by the end of 1933, AT&T owned almost 94 percent of the

nation's 82,086,828 total miles of wire, produced over 87 percent of the 15,400,000 telephones in the country, and employed nearly 90 percent of all telephone workers. See *Economic Notes* (New York: Labor Research Association), May 1935, 8.

21. Dan Schiller, "The Hidden History of US Public Service Telecommunications, 1919–1956," *Info* 9, nos. 2–3 (2007): 18.

22. For an early history of the FCC and radio broadcasting that documents how the medium became so commercialized from its inception, see Robert McChesney, *Telecommunications, Mass Media & Democracy: The Battle for the Control of U.S. Broadcasting, 1928–1935* (New York: Oxford University Press, 1993).

23. Quoted in Pickard, *America's Battle for Media Democracy,* 38.

24. Communications Act, 47 U.S.C. § 201(b) (1934).

25. Communications Act, 47 U.S.C. § 202(a) (1934). I thank Kevin Taglang for pointing out these quotes.

26. For more details regarding the Walker Report, see Victor Pickard, "A Giant Besieged: AT&T, an Activist FCC, and Contestation in Corporate-State Relations, 1935–1939" (paper presented at the Union for Democratic Communications, St. Louis, April 22–25, 2004). For an earlier muckraking account, see N. R. Danielian, *AT&T: The Story of Industrial Conquest* (New York: Vanguard, 1939).

27. "$750,000 Fund for A.T. & T. Investigation Wins the Approval of Senate Committee," *New York Times,* February 6, 1935, 29; "Roosevelt Orders Telephone Inquiry," *New York Times,* March 16, 1935, 21.

28. Robert Britt Horwitz, *The Irony of Regulatory Reform* (New York: Oxford University Press, 1989), 137.

29. *Economic Notes* (New York: Labor Research Association), July 1939, 10.

30. For a discussion of natural monopolies, see Eli Noam, "Is Cable

Television a Natural Monopoly?" *Communications: International Journal of Communications Research* 9, nos. 2–3 (1984): 241–59; Robert Babe, *Telecommunications in Canada* (Toronto: University of Toronto Press, 1990), 137–50; C. Edwin Baker, *Media, Markets, and Democracy* (Cambridge: Cambridge University Press, 2001), 35; Crawford, *Captive Audience,* 37–38.

31. Starr points out that although an 1894 Supreme Court case established nondiscrimination, it was only in 1910 that Congress amended the Interstate Commerce Act to unambiguously define telephone and telegraph companies as common carriers. See Starr, *The Creation of the Media,* 188.

32. Milton Mueller and other revisionist historians have pointed out that a self-interested AT&T happily embraced the idea of "universal service" to argue that only one system under one regulatory regime was needed. The phrase itself became a kind of public relations slogan for the Bell system. See Milton Mueller, "The Telephone War: Interconnection, Competition, and Monopoly in the Making of Universal Telephone Service" (PhD diss., University of Pennsylvania, 1989), 160. See generally John, *Network Nation,* 340–69. Smaller, local carriers, including rural co-ops, also played a key role in building out to remote communities.

33. For a comprehensive scholarly analysis, see Robert Cannon, "The Legacy of the Federal Communications Commission's Computer Inquiries," *Federal Communications Law Journal* 55, no. 2 (2002): 167–206. For a discussion of how the FCC's Computer Inquiries relate to net neutrality, see Becky Lentz, "Excavating Historicity in the U.S. Network Neutrality Debate: An Interpretive Perspective on Policy Change," *Communication, Culture & Critique* 6, no. 4 (2013): 568–97.

34. These examples are used in Robinson Meyer, "Antonin Scalia Totally Gets Net Neutrality," *Atlantic*, May 16, 2014, https://www .theatlantic.com/technology/archive/2014/05/net-neutralitys -little-known-hero-antonin-scalia/361315/.

35. We thank Dan Schiller for sharing this analysis with us. He discusses this history in Dan Schiller, *Telematics and Government* (Norwood, NJ: Ablex, 1982), 22–41.

36. S. Derek Turner of Free Press argues that the Telecom Act, to the extent that it engaged with the internet, actually held some pro-competition initiatives, but industry lobbyists were able to prevent them from ever being actualized. See *Changing Media: Public Interest Policies for the Digital Age* (Washington, DC: Free Press, 2009).

37. Parts of this section draw from Victor Pickard and Pawel Popiel, "The Media Democracy Agenda: The Strategy and Legacy of FCC Commissioner Michael J. Copps," Evanston, IL: Benton Foundation, 2018.

38. Michael Copps, "Dissenting Statement of Commissioner Michael J. Copps, in the Matter of Inquiry concerning High-Speed Access to the Internet over Cable and Other Facilities Internet over Cable Declaratory Order Proceeding Appropriate Regulatory Treatment for Broadband Access to the Internet over Cable Facilities GN No. 00-185," 2002, https://transition .fcc.gov/Speeches/Copps/Statements/2002/stmjc210.html.

39. Christopher Stern, "FCC Gives Cable Firms Net Rights," *Washington Post*, March 15, 2002.

40. Michael Copps, "Remarks of Michael J. Copps, Federal Communications Commissioner: 'The Beginning of the End of the

Internet? Discrimination, Closed Networks, and the Future of Cyberspace,'" New America Foundation, Washington, DC, October 9, 2003, https://docs.fcc.gov/public/attachments /DOC-239800A1.pdf.

41. Ted Hearn, "Cable-Modem Appeal Denied by Ninth Circuit," *Multichannel News*, April 1, 2004, https://www.multichannel .com/news/cable-modem-appeal-denied-ninth-circuit-270836.

42. For a discussion of this decision, particularly how its aftermath played out on Capitol Hill, see Victor Pickard, "After Net Neutrality," *LSE Media Policy Project*, July 18, 2016, http://blogs.lse .ac.uk/mediapolicyproject/2016/07/18/after-net-neutrality/.

43. National Cable & Telecommunications Association v. Brand X Internet Services, 545 U.S. 967 (2005).

44. Michael Copps, "Concurring Statement of Commissioner Michael J. Copps Re: Preserving the Open Internet, GN Docket No. 09-191, Broadband Industry Practices, WC Docket No. 07-52," 2010; Federal Communications Commission, Policy Statement, "Appropriate Framework for Broadband Access to the Internet over Wireline Facilities," CC Docket No. 05-151, 2005, https://docs.fcc.gov/public/attachments/FCC-05–151A1.pdf.

45. Robert McDowell, "Who Should Solve This Internet Crisis?" *Washington Post*, July 28, 2008. Some anti–net neutrality activists tried to cast net neutrality as a government intrusion. Leading libertarian policy analyst Adam D. Thierer referred to net neutrality as "a fairness doctrine for the internet." See "A Fairness Doctrine for the Internet," *City Journal*, October 18, 2007, https://www.city-journal.org/html/fairness-doctrine -internet-10315.html.

46. Craig Aaron, "Cracking Down on Comcast," *Guardian,* July 16, 2008, https://www.theguardian.com/commentisfree/2008/jul/16/internet.cablewirelessbusiness.

47. Karl Bode, "Comcast Responds to Traffic Shaping Accusations," *DSL Reports,* August 21, 2007, http://www.dslreports.com/shownews/Comcast-Responds-To-Traffic-Shaping-Accusations-86816.

48. Dan Frommer, "Comcast's Supporters at FCC Meeting: Paid, Asleep," *Business Insider,* February 26, 2008, https://www.businessinsider.com/2008/2/comcasts-supporters-at-fcc-meeting-paid-sleeping-strangers.

49. Broadband Industry Practices, Petition of Free Press *et al.* for Declaratory Ruling That Degrading an Internet Application Violates the FCC's Internet Policy Statement and Does Not Meet an Exception for "Reasonable Network Management," WC Docket No. 07-52; *Memorandum Opinion and Order,* FCC 08-183 (August 1, 2008).

50. Comcast Corp. v. FCC, 600 F.3d 642 (DC Cir. 2010).

51. Quoted in Cecilia Kang, "FCC's Copps: Net Neutrality Requires Reclassification of Broadband," *Washington Post,* December 3, 2010, http://voices.washingtonpost.com/posttech/2010/12/fccs_copps_net_neutrality_requ.html.

52. Michael Copps, "Statement of Commissioner Michael J. Copps on Chairman Genachowski's Announcement to Reclassify Broadband," *Federal Communications Commission,* May 6, 2010, https://docs.fcc.gov/public/attachments/DOC-297946A1.pdf.

53. Verizon v. FCC, 740 F.3d 623 (DC Cir. 2014). The Open Internet Order, issued shortly after the Comcast decision, had

endeavored to protect net neutrality by requiring transparency and prohibiting blocking and unreasonable discrimination by ISPs.

54. Edward Wyatt, "F.C.C., in a Shift, Backs Fast Lanes for Web Traffic," *New York Times*, April 23, 2014, https://www.nytimes.com/2014/04/24/technology/fcc-new-net-neutrality-rules.html.

55. Marvin Ammori, "The Case for Net Neutrality: What's Wrong with Obama's Internet Policy," *Foreign Affairs*, June 16, 2014, https://www.foreignaffairs.com/articles/united-states/2014-06-16/case-net-neutrality.

56. Michael Copps, "The Biggest FCC Vote Ever," *Benton Foundation*, January 6, 2015, https://www.benton.org/blog/biggest-fcc-vote-ever.

57. Jose Pagliery, "AT&T: We're Going to Sue the Government," *CNN Business*, February 4, 2015, https://money.cnn.com/2015/02/04/technology/att-fcc-letter/. The NCTA, CTIA, American Cable Association, and USTelecom also sued to overturn the FCC's decision.

58. Cecilia Kang, "Court Backs Rules Treating Internet as Utility, Not Luxury," *New York Times*, June 14, 2016, https://www.nytimes.com/2016/06/15/technology/net-neutrality-fcc-appeals-court-ruling.html.

59. This historic turn is discussed in Victor Pickard, "It's Not Too Late to Save Net Neutrality from a Captured FCC," *Nation*, May 5, 2017, https://www.thenation.com/article/its-not-too-late-to-save-net-neutrality-from-a-captured-fcc/.

60. Jim Puzzanghera, "Trump Names New FCC Chairman: Ajit Pai, Who Wants to Take a 'Weed Whacker' to Net Neutrality," *Los*

Angeles Times, January 23, 2017, http://www.latimes.com/business/la-fi-pai-fcc-chairman-20170123-story.html.

61. Cecilia Kang, "F.C.C. Chairman Pushes Sweeping Changes to Net Neutrality Rules," *New York Times,* April 26, 2017, https://www.nytimes.com/2017/04/26/technology/net-neutrality.html.

62. Kaleigh Rogers, "99.7 Percent of Unique FCC Comments Favored Net Neutrality," *Motherboard,* October 15, 2018, https://motherboard.vice.com/en_us/article/3kmedj/997-percent-of-unique-fcc-comments-favored-net-neutrality.

63. Dell Cameron, "FCC Emails Show Agency Spread Lies to Bolster Dubious DDoS Attack Claims," *Gizmodo,* June 5, 2018, https://gizmodo.com/fcc-emails-show-agency-spread-lies-to-bolster-dubious-d-1826535344.

64. FCC, "FCC Releases Restoring Internet Freedom Order," December 14, 2017, https://www.fcc.gov/document/fcc-releases-restoring-internet-freedom-order.

65. This is documented in Meinrath and Pickard, "The New Network Neutrality." See also Meinrath and Pickard, "Transcending Net Neutrality."

66. Nunziato, *Virtual Freedom,* 5–6.

67. Nunziato, *Virtual Freedom,* 7.

68. Geoff Boucher, "AT&T: Pearl Jam Mute a 'Mistake,'" *Los Angeles Times,* August 10, 2007, http://articles.latimes.com/2007/aug/10/entertainment/et-quick10.s3.

69. Timothy Karr, "Net Neutrality Violations: A Brief History," *Free Press,* January 24, 2018, https://www.freepress.net/our-response/expert-analysis/explainers/net-neutrality-violations-brief-history.

1. Thomas Streeter, *The Net Effect: Romanticism, Capitalism, and the Internet,* Critical Cultural Communication (New York: New York University Press, 2011), 106–15; Megan Sapnar Ankerson, *Dot-Com Design: The Rise of a Usable, Social, Commercial Web,* Critical Cultural Communication (New York: New York University Press, 2018).

2. White House, "The Framework for Global Electronic Commerce," July 1, 1997, https://clintonwhitehouse4.archives.gov/WH/New/Commerce/read.html.

3. "How the Internet Killed the Phone Business," *Economist,* September 15, 2005, https://www.economist.com/leaders/2005/09/15/how-the-internet-killed-the-phone-business.

4. Reza Dibadj, "Competitive Debacle in Local Telephony: Is the 1996 Telecommunications Act to Blame?" *Washington University Law Review* 81, no. 1 (2003): 14–15.

5. Tom Downes and Shane Greenstein, "Universal Access and Local Internet Markets in the US," *Research Policy* 31, no. 7 (2002): 1035–52.

6. See Yochai Benkler et al., "Next Generation Connectivity: A Review of Broadband Internet Transitions and Policy from around the World." This 2010 report was commissioned by the FCC and conducted by a team of researchers led by Yochai Benkler at the Berkman Center for Internet & Society at Harvard University.

7. See Rob Frieden, "Lessons from Broadband Development in Canada, Japan, Korea and the United States," *Telecommunications Policy* 29, no. 8 (2005): 602.

8. Mark Cooper, "Open Communications Platforms: The Physical Infrastructure as the Bedrock of Innovation and Democratic Discourse in the Internet Age," *Journal on Telecommunications and High Technology Law* 2 (2003): 223.

9. We defer to the Federal Communications Commission's current standard for what constitutes broadband internet: a minimum download speed of at least twenty-five Mbps and a minimum upload speed of at least three Mbps. See Federal Communications Commission, "Internet Access Services: Status as of June 30, 2017," Washington, DC: November 2018, https://docs.fcc.gov/public/attachments/DOC-355166A1 .pdf.

10. Adam D. Thierer and Clyde Wayne Crews, *What's Yours Is Mine: Open Access and the Rise of Infrastructure Socialism* (Washington, DC: Cato Institute, 2003).

11. Ted Hearn, "Powell: 'Scream' at Forced Access," *Multichannel*, October 26, 2001, https://www.multichannel.com/news/powell -scream-forced-access-155848.

12. Jonathan E. Nuechterlein and Philip J. Weiser, *Digital Crossroads: Telecommunications Law and Policy in the Internet Age* (Cambridge, MA: MIT Press, 2013), 418.

13. See Tim Wu, "Wireless Carterfone," *International Journal of Communication* 1 (2007): 389–426.

14. This often-neglected policy history is discussed in John Bergmayer, "We Need Title II Protections in the Uncompetitive Broadband Market," *Public Knowledge*, April 26, 2017, https:// www.publicknowledge.org/news-blog/blogs/we-need-title-ii -protections-in-the-uncompetitive-broadband-market.

15. Amitai Etzioni, *Moral Dimension: Toward a New Economics* (New York: Free Press, 1988), 218.

16. Tim Wu, *The Attention Merchants: The Epic Scramble to Get inside Our Heads* (New York: Knopf, 2016).

17. Ben H. Bagdikian, *The New Media Monopoly* (Boston: Beacon, 2004), 137–38.

18. Andrew Jay Schwartzman, Cheryl A. Leanza, and Harold Feld, "The Legal Case for Diversity in Broadcast Ownership," in *The Future of Media: Resistance and Reform in the 21st Century,* ed. Robert W. McChesney, Russell Newman, and Ben Scott (New York: Seven Stories, 2005), 149–50.

19. Rani Molla, "A Merged T-Mobile and Sprint Will Still Be Smaller Than AT&T or Verizon," *Recode,* April 30, 2018, https://www.recode.net/2018/4/30/17300652/tmobile-sprint-att-verizon-merger-wireless-subscriber-chart.

20. Crawford, *Captive Audience,* 16.

21. Hannah Trostle and Christopher Mitchell, "Profiles of Monopoly: Big Cable & Telecom," Minneapolis: Institute for Local Self-Reliance, July 31, 2018, https://ilsr.org/monopoly-networks/.

22. Wu, *The Master Switch,* 247.

23. Rob Bluey, "Q&A: FCC Chairman Ajit Pai on Repealing Obama's Net Neutrality Rules," *Daily Signal,* November 21, 2017, https://www.dailysignal.com/2017/11/21/qa-fcc-chairman-explains-hes-ending-obamas-heavy-handed-internet-regulations/.

24. Adam Smith, *The Wealth of Nations: Books I–III,* ed. Andrew S. Skinner (London: Penguin Books, 1999), 232.

25. Quoted in Mark Cooper, *Media Ownership and Democracy in the Digital Information Age: Promoting Diversity with First Amend-*

ment Principles and Market Structure Analysis (Stanford, CA: Center for Internet & Society, Stanford Law School, 2003), 114.

26. Robert McChesney discusses the "ISP cartel" in *Digital Disconnect: How Capitalism Is Turning the Internet against Democracy* (New York: New Press, 2013), 115–19. See also Robert McChesney, "Be Realistic, Demand the Impossible: Three Radically Democratic Internet Policies," in *The Future of Internet Policy,* ed. Peter Decherney and Victor Pickard (New York: Routledge, 2016), 40–41.

27. Jon Brodkin, "Comcast Says It's Too Expensive to Compete against Other Cable Companies," *Ars Technica,* September 24, 2014, https://arstechnica.com/information-technology/2014/09/comcast-says-its-too-expensive-to-compete-against-other-cable-companies/. For a political and economic history of Comcast's rise to power, see Lee McGuigan and Victor Pickard, "The Political Economy of Comcast," in *Global Media Giants,* ed. Ben Birkinbine, Rodrigo Gómez García, and Janet Wasko (New York: Routledge, 2016), 72–91.

28. Trostle and Mitchell, "Profiles of Monopoly."

29. Susan Crawford, "The Looming Cable Monopoly," *Yale Law & Policy Review,* June 1, 2010, https://ylpr.yale.edu/inter_alia/looming-cable-monopoly.

30. Cynthia Littleton, "Charter to Become Second-Largest Cable Operator in Divestiture Pact with Comcast," *Variety,* April 28, 2014, https://variety.com/2014/tv/news/charter-to-become-second-largest-cable-operator-in-divestiture-pact-with-comcast-1201165594/.

31. Philip J. Reny and Michael A. Williams, "The Deterrent Effect

of Cable System Clustering on Overbuilders: An Economic Analysis of *Behrend v. Comcast*," *Economics Bulletin* 35, no. 1 (2015): 519–27.

32. Roger Cheng, "Verizon to End Rollout of FiOS," *Wall Street Journal*, March 30, 2010, http://www.wsj.com/articles/SB 10001424052702303410404575151773432729614.

33. Nathan Ingraham, "Verizon Wireless' Partnership with Comcast Sets Up Potential Conflicts with FiOS," *Verge*, January 31, 2012, https://www.theverge.com/2012/1/31/2761023/verizon -wireless-comcast-partnership-fios-xfinity-conflict.

34. Federal Communications Commission, "Internet Access Services: Status as of December 31, 2016," 6.

35. "A Third of U.S. Households Have Three or More Smartphones," *Pew Research Center*, May 25, 2017, http://www.pewresearch.org /fact-tank/2017/05/25/a-third-of-americans-live-in-a-household -with-three-or-more-smartphones/.

36. "OECD Fixed Broadband Basket, High User," Organisation for Economic Co-operation and Development, June 2017, http:// www.oecd.org/sti/broadband/4.10.FBB-High_2017.xls.

37. "State of the Internet Q1 2017," Akamai, 2017, https://www .akamai.com/fr/fr/multimedia/documents/state-of-the-internet /q1–2017-state-of-the-internet-connectivity-report.pdf.

38. Susan Crawford, *Fiber: The Coming Tech Revolution—and Why America Might Miss It* (New Haven, CT: Yale University Press, 2018), 39.

39. Nick Russo et al., "The Cost of Connectivity 2014," Washington, DC: New America Foundation, October 2014, https://www

.newamerica.org/oti/policy-papers/the-cost-of-connectivity
-2014/.

40. "OECD Fixed Broadband Basket, High User."

41. Benkler et al., "Next Generation Connectivity"; Christopher T.
Marsden, "Comparative Case Studies in Implementing Net
Neutrality: A Critical Analysis of Zero Rating," *SCRIPTed* 13,
no. 1 (May 2016): 1–39.

42. Timothy Karr, "Net Neutrality Violations: A Brief History," *Free
Press,* January 24, 2018, https://www.freepress.net/our-response
/expert-analysis/explainers/net-neutrality-violations-brief
-history.

43. See, for example, Shalini Ramachandran, "Cord-Cutting: Cable's
Offer You Can't Refuse," *Wall Street Journal,* November 13,
2012, https://www.wsj.com/articles/SB10001424127887324
07350457810951366098932. Most egregiously, in 2013 Time
Warner generated a 97 percent profit margin on high-speed
internet. This was revealed by Bruce Kushnick in "Time Warner
Cable's 97 Percent Profit Margin on High-Speed Internet
Service Exposed," *Huffington Post,* February 2, 2015, https://
www.huffingtonpost.com/bruce-kushnick/time-warner-cables
-97-pro_b_6591916.html.

44. Susan Crawford and Ben Scott, "Be Careful What You Wish For:
Why Europe Should Avoid the Mistakes of US Internet Access
Policy," Berlin: Stiftung Neue Verantwortung, June 2015,
https://www.stiftung-nv.de/sites/default/files/us-eu.internet
.access.policy.pdf.

45. Charter Communications, "Charter Announces Fourth Quarter

and Full Year 2017 Results," February 2, 2018, https://news room.charter.com/press-releases/charter-announces-fourth -quarter-and-full-year-2017-results/.

46. Martin Baccardax, "Comcast Tops Q4 Profit Estimates, Boosts Dividend and Stock Buyback Plans," *TheStreet,* January 24, 2018, https://www.thestreet.com/story/14460395/1/comcast -tops-q4-earnings-estimates-boosts-dividend-and-buyback-plans .html. For a broader economic history of Comcast, see Mc-Guigan and Pickard, "The Political Economy of Comcast."

CHAPTER 3. THE MAKING OF A MOVEMENT

1. Josh Breitbart, "You Can't Be Moving on a Neutral Train," *Civil Defense,* April 19, 2006, https://breitbart.wordpress.com/2006 /04/19/you-cant-be-moving-on-a-neutral-train/; Arianna Huffington, "'Net Neutrality': Why Are the Bad Guys So Much Better at Naming Things?" *Huffington Post,* May 3, 2006, https://www.huffingtonpost.com/arianna-huffington/net -neutrality-why-are-th_b_20311.html.

2. Ken Fisher, "Poll: Americans Don't Want Net Neutrality (or Maybe They Don't Know What It Is)," *Ars Technica,* September 18, 2008, https://arstechnica.com/tech-policy/2006/09/7772/.

3. Robert D. Atkinson, Daniel Castro, and Alan McQuinn, "How Tech Populism Is Undermining Innovation," Information Technology and Innovation Foundation, April 2015, 1, https:// itif.org/publications/2015/04/01/how-tech-populism-under mining-innovation. For a more in-depth analysis of the convergence of populist political logics and policy, see Danny Kimball, "Wonkish Populism in Media Advocacy and Net

Neutrality Policy Making," *International Journal of Communication* 10 (2016): 5949–68.

4. Arshad Mohammed, "SBC Head Ignites Access Debate," *Washington Post*, November 4, 2005, http://www.washingtonpost.com/wp-dyn/content/article/2005/11/03/AR2005110302211.html.

5. In the spirit of full disclosure, one of the authors, Victor Pickard, worked at Free Press in 2009 and now sits on the organization's board.

6. Robert D. Atkinson and Philip J. Weiser, "A Third Way on Network Neutrality," *New Atlantis: A Journal of Technology & Society* (Summer 2006): 50.

7. Jeffrey A. Hart, "The Net Neutrality Debate in the United States," *Journal of Information Technology & Politics* 8, no. 4 (2011): 425.

8. "Building the Internet Toll Road," *Wired*, February 26, 2006, https://www.wired.com/2006/02/building-the-internet-toll-road/. For a discussion about Free Press and Save the Internet coalition, see The Communicators, "Ben Scott on Net Neutrality," *C-SPAN*, 2007, https://www.youtube.com/watch?v=ladtEC-G7pU.

9. Ernesto Laclau, *On Populist Reason* (London: Verso, 2005), 117.

10. *Save the Internet! Independence Day*, 2006, https://www.youtube.com/watch?v=cWtoXUocViE. At various points throughout the net neutrality saga, industry groups funded "astroturf" organizations to help create the perception of popular agitation against net neutrality. One of the earliest of these was called Hands Off the Internet. See Meinrath and Pickard, "The New Network Neutrality," 227.

11. "Your Own Personal Internet," *Wired,* June 30, 2006, https:// www.wired.com/2006/06/your-own-person/. Bill Herman, an intern at Public Knowledge, was the person responsible for the original recording of Senator Stevens's rant.

12. *The Daily Show* with Jon Stewart, "Headlines—Internet," Comedy Central video clip, July 2006, http://www.cc.com/video-clips /u01ore/the-daily-show-with-jon-stewart-headlines—internet.

13. "Sen. Ted Stevens—Alaska," Open Secrets, accessed October 28, 2018, https://www.opensecrets.org/members-of-congress /contributors?cid=N00007997&cycle=2008&type=C.

14. Peter Dahlgren, *The Political Web: Media, Participation and Alternative Democracy* (Basingstoke, UK: Palgrave Macmillan, 2013), 139.

15. Quoted in Christopher T. Marsden, *Net Neutrality: Towards a Coregulatory Solution* (London: Bloomsbury Academic, 2010), 1.

16. Nancy Scola and Alex Byers, "FCC's Win Cements Obama's Internet Legacy," *Politico,* June 14, 2016, https://politi.co/2TSdgaL.

17. "Google-Verizon Pact Worse Than Feared," *Free Press,* August 9, 2010, https://www.freepress.net/news/press-releases/google -verizon-pact-worse-feared.

18. Marvin Ammori, "Google-Verizon Pact: Makes BP Look Good," *Huffington Post,* August 10, 2010, https://www.huffingtonpost .com/marvin-ammori/google-verizon-pact-makes_b_677296 .html.

19. Sergey Brin, "Search Engines, Technology, and Business" (lecture delivered at the University of California, Berkeley, October 3, 2005).

20. "Techies Score Victory on Net Neutrality," *NBC News,* February

26, 2015, https://www.nbcnews.com/tech/internet/techies
-score-victory-net-neutrality-n313406.

21. Craig Aaron, personal communication, December 4, 2018.

22. Battle for the Net, "We Are Team Internet," accessed September 3, 2018, https://www.battleforthenet.com/teaminternet.

23. Brody Mullins and Gautham Nagesh, "Jostling Begins as FCC's Net Neutrality Vote Nears," *Wall Street Journal*, February 24, 2015.

24. Battle for the Net, accessed October 13, 2018, https://www
.battleforthenet.com.

25. Bob Lannon, "What Can We Learn from 800,000 Public Comments on the FCC's Net Neutrality Plan?" Sunlight Foundation, 2014, https://sunlightfoundation.com/2014/09/02/what-can
-we-learn-from-800000-public-comments-on-the-fccs-net
-neutrality-plan/.

26. Battle for the Net, "Sept. 10th Is the Internet Slowdown," 2014, https://www.battleforthenet.com/sept10th/.

27. Fight for the Future, "Press Release: The Internet Slowdown by the Numbers," September 11, 2014, http://tumblr.fightforthe
future.org/post/97225186398/press-release-the-internet-slow
down-by-the.

28. Ashley Killough, "Net Neutrality Protesters Confront FCC Chairman," *CNN*, November 11, 2014, http://www.cnn.com
/2014/11/11/politics/fcc-chairman-protesters/index.html.

29. Soraya Nadia McDonald, "John Oliver's Net Neutrality Rant May Have Caused FCC Site Crash," *Washington Post*, June 4, 2014, https://www.washingtonpost.com/news/morning-mix
/wp/2014/06/04/john-olivers-net-neutrality-rant-may-have
-caused-fcc-site-crash/.

30. Robert Faris et al., "The Role of the Networked Public Sphere in the US Net Neutrality Policy Debate," *International Journal of Communication* 10 (2016): 5849.

31. Amy Schatz, "FCC's Wheeler on Viral Net Neutrality Video: 'I Am Not a Dingo,'" *Recode*, June 13, 2014, https://www.recode .net/2014/6/13/11627962/fccs-wheeler-on-viral-net-neutrality -video-i-am-not-a-dingo.

32. Alex T. Williams and Martin Shelton, "What Drove Spike in Public Comments on Net Neutrality? Likely, a Comedian," Washington, DC: Pew Research Center, 2014, http://www .pewresearch.org/fact-tank/2014/09/05/what-drove-spike-in -public-comments-on-net-neutrality-likely-a-comedian/.

33. @FCC, "We've been experiencing technical difficulties . . .," *Twitter*, June 2, 2014, https://twitter.com/FCC/status/47356 5753463959552.

34. *President Obama's Statement on Keeping the Internet Open and Free—YouTube*, November 10, 2014, https://www.youtube.com /watch?v=uKcjQPVwfDk.

35. There has been some speculation as to why Obama intervened when and how he did. One theory is that passing net neutrality had been on Obama's so-called f**k-it list, and now that the great distraction of the midterms was over, he could focus on this priority, which had remained dormant for much of his presidency.

36. "Overwhelming Bipartisan Majority Opposes Repealing Net Neutrality," Washington, DC: Program for Public Consultation at the University of Maryland, 2017, http://www.publicconsul

tation.org/united-states/overwhelming-bipartisan-majority
-opposes-repealing-net-neutrality/.

37. Elizabeth Stinson, "Day of Action: How Facebook, Google, and More Supported Net Neutrality," *Wired*, July 12, 2017, https:// www.wired.com/story/day-of-action-internet-protests-google -facebook-reddit/.

38. @HamillHimself, "Cute video Ajit 'Aren't I Precious?' Pai—but you are profoundly unworthy 2 wield a lightsaber—a Jedi acts selflessly for the common man—NOT lie 2 enrich giant corporations. Btw—did you pay John Williams his royalty? @AjitPai FCCorpShill #AJediYouAreNOT," *Twitter*, December 16, 2017, https://twitter.com/hamillhimself/status/941984701085925 376?lang=en.

39. Brian Feldman, "Ajit Pai Made a 'Viral' Video with a Wannabe Pizzagater as a Last-Ditch Attempt to Defend New Internet Rules," *New York Magazine*, December 14, 2017, http://nymag .com/intelligencer/2017/12/ajit-pais-pizzagater-martina-markota -hates-net-neutrality.html; Tom McKay, "Ajit Pai Thinks You're Stupid Enough to Buy This Crap [Update: One of the 7 Things Is Dancing with a Pizzagater]," *Gizmodo*, December 13, 2017, https://gizmodo.com/ajit-pai-thinks-youre-stupid-enough-to -buy-this-crap-1821277398.

40. Tony Romm, "Netflix CEO: Net Neutrality Is No Longer Our 'Primary Battle,'" *Recode*, May 31, 2017, https://www.recode.net /2017/5/31/15720268/netflix-ceo-reed-hastings-net-neutrality -open-internet.

41. Klint Finley, "This Hearing May Decide the Future of Net

Neutrality," *Wired*, February 1, 2019, https://www.wired.com
/story/this-hearing-decide-future-net-neutrality/.

42. Katharine Trendacosta, "Victory! California Passes Net Neutrality Bill," *Electronic Frontier Foundation*, August 31, 2018, https://
www.eff.org/deeplinks/2018/08/victory-california-passes-net
-neutrality-bill.

43. Karl Bode, "Why Feds Can't Block California's Net Neutrality
Bill," *Verge*, October 2, 2018, https://www.theverge.com/2018
/10/2/17927430/california-net-neutrality-law-preemption
-state-lawsuit.

44. Heath Kelly, "California Just Passed Its Net Neutrality Law. The
DOJ Is Already Suing," *CNN Business*, October 1, 2018, https://
www.cnn.com/2018/10/01/tech/california-net-neutrality-law
/index.html.

45. Christopher Hooton, "An Empirical Investigation of the
Impacts of Net Neutrality," The Internet Association, 2017, 3,
https://internetassociation.org/publications/an-empirical
-investigation-of-the-impacts-of-net-neutrality/.

46 "Malkia Cyril on Why Net Neutrality Is a Civil Rights Issue,"
NBC News, December 8, 2017, https://www.nbcnews.com
/feature/debunker/video/malkia-cyril-on-why-net-neutrality
-is-a-civil-rights-issue-1112468547817.

47. "Civil Rights and Media Justice Leaders Join Internet-Wide Day
of Action for Net Neutrality on July 12th," Oakland: Center for
Media Justice, July 12, 2017, https://centerformediajustice.org
/2017/07/12/civil-rights-media-justice-leaders-join-internet
-wide-day-action-net-neutrality-july-12th/.

1. William M. Emmons, "Franklin D. Roosevelt, Electric Utilities, and the Power of Competition," *Journal of Economic History* 53, no. 4 (1993): 883.

2. Richard Martin, *Coal Wars: The Future of Energy and the Fate of the Planet* (New York: Palgrave Macmillan, 2015), 17.

3. These approaches correspond to three general methods to contain monopolies in particular and commercialism in general, discussed in Victor Pickard, *Democracy without Journalism? The Rise of the Misinformation Society* (New York: Oxford University Press, 2019).

4. For an incisive analysis of America's anti-monopoly movement, see Tim Wu's recent book, *The Curse of Bigness: Antitrust in the New Gilded Age* (New York: Columbia Global Reports, 2018).

5. It is important to point out that these are not mutually exclusive measures; many would argue that we need to wield both antitrust *and* public interest regulation.

6. Michael O'Rielly, "Muni Broadband's Ominous Threat to the First Amendment," Federal Communications Commission, December 13, 2018, https://www.fcc.gov/news-events/blog/2018/12/13/muni-broadbands-ominous-threat-first-amendment.

7. Quoted in Emmons, "Franklin D. Roosevelt, Electric Utilities, and the Power of Competition," 884.

8. For an excellent resource that includes maps and data about community/municipal broadband, see the Institute for Local Self-Reliance's "Community Network Map," Community Networks, January 2019, https://muninetworks.org/community

map; Klint Finley, "Brits Approach (True) Speed of Light over Fiber Cable," *Wired,* March 28, 2013, https://www.wired.com /2013/03/internet-at-the-speed-of-light/.

9. James K. Wilcox, "People Still Don't Like Their Cable Companies," *Consumer Reports,* August 8, 2018, https://www .consumerreports.org/phone-tv-internet-bundles/people-still -dont-like-their-cable-companies-telecom-survey/.

10. David Talbot, Kira Hessekiel, and Danielle Kehl, "Community-Owned Fiber Networks: Value Leaders in America," Cambridge, MA: Berkman Klein Center for Internet & Society, 2017, http:// nrs.harvard.edu/urn-3:HUL.InstRepos:34623859.

11. Lisa Gonzalez, "Totals Are In: Comcast Spends $900K in Fort Collins Election," *Community Networks,* December 9, 2017, https://muninetworks.org/content/totals-are-comcast-spends -900k-fort-collins-election.

12. "Municipal Broadband Is Roadblocked or Outlawed in 26 States," *Broadband Now,* April 17, 2019, https://broadbandnow .com/report/municipal-broadband-roadblocks/.

13. Monica Anderson and John B. Horrigan, "Americans Have Mixed Views on Policies Encouraging Broadband Adoption," Pew Research Center, April 10, 2017, http://www.pewresearch .org/fact-tank/2017/04/10/americans-have-mixed-views-on -policies-encouraging-broadband-adoption/.

14. Alex Shephard, "A Public Option for the Internet," *New Republic,* May 8, 2018, https://newrepublic.com/article/148330 /public-option-internet.

15. Evan Malmgren, "Could Vermont Become the First State with Universal Broadband?" *Nation,* October 26, 2018, https://www

.thenation.com/article/could-vermont-become-the-first-state
-with-universal-broadband/.

16. "Polling the Left Agenda," Data for Progress, 2018, https://
www.dataforprogress.org/polling-the-left-agenda/.

17. Roger Lowenstein, "The 'Noble Art' of Governing: A Practical
Agenda for the House," *Washington Post,* November 14, 2018,
https://www.washingtonpost.com/business/economy/the
-noble-art-of-governing-a-practical-agenda-for-the-house/2018
/11/14/81150b1e-e787–11e8-b8dc-66cca409c180_story.html
?utm_term=.c9c27725976a.

18. For further discussion of the challenges of respecting user privacy on public internet networks, see E. Casey Lide, "Balancing
the Benefits and Privacy Concerns of Municipal Broadband
Applications," *NYU Journal of Legislation & Public Policy* 11, no. 3
(2007): 467–93; and Jay Stanley, "The Public Internet Option:
How Local Governments Can Provide Network Neutrality,
Privacy, and Access for All," American Civil Liberties Union,
March 2018, https://www.aclu.org/report/public-internet
-option.

19. For a comprehensive overview of literature on regulatory cap-
tures, see Adam Thierer, "Regulatory Capture: What the Experts
Have Found," *Technology Liberation Front,* December 19, 2010,
https://techliberation.com/2010/12/19/regulatory-capture-what
-the-experts-have-found/.

20. Craig Aaron and Timothy Karr of Free Press, personal corre-
spondence, July 27, 2018.

21. Jon Brodkin, "FCC's Revolving Door: Former Chairman Leads
Charge against Title II," *Ars Technica,* April 14, 2015, https://

arstechnica.com/information-technology/2015/04/fccs
-revolving-door-former-chairman-leads-charge-against-title-ii/.

22. Tim Karr, "FCC Commissioner Cashes in at Your Expense," *Common Dreams,* May 14, 2011, https://www.commondreams .org/views/2011/05/14/fcc-commissioner-cashes-your-expense.

23. Even Mignon Clyburn, who was a staunch ally of consumer and public interest groups during her tenure as FCC commissioner from 2009 to 2018, was hired by T-Mobile in February 2019 to advise the company on its pending mega-merger with Sprint. See Brian Fung, "Mignon Clyburn, Former FCC Commissioner, Hired by T-Mobile to 'Advise' on Sprint Merger," *Washington Post,* February 6, 2019, https://www.washingtonpost.com /technology/2019/02/06/t-mobile-gains-powerful-ally-hiring -former-fcc-commissioner-advise-its-sprint-merger/?utm_term =.e60ca665841e.

24. As a congressional staffer, Victor Pickard experienced firsthand the embeddedness of corporate lobbyists in the halls of govern-ment power, and how this affected the net neutrality debate immediately after the *Brand X* decision. See "After Net Neutral-ity," *LSE Media Policy Project,* July 18, 2016, http://blogs.lse.ac .uk/mediapolicyproject/2016/07/18/after-net-neutrality/, re-printed on *Huffington Post,* July 20, 2016, http://www.huffington post.com/victor-pickard/after-net-neutrality_b_11043316.html.

25. Pickard, *America's Battle for Media Democracy,* 218.

26. Victor Pickard, "The Return of the Nervous Liberals: Market Fundamentalism, Policy Failure, and Recurring Journalism Crises," *Communication Review* 18, no. 2 (2015): 82–97; Dwayne Winseck and Jefferson D. Pooley, "A Curious Tale of Economics

and Common Carriage (Net Neutrality) at the FCC: A Reply to
Faulhaber, Singer, and Urschel," *International Journal of Communication* 11 (2017): 2702–33.

27. Jedediah Purdy, "Neoliberal Constitutionalism: Lochnerism for
a New Economy," *Law & Contemporary Problems* 77, no. 4 (2014):
197.

28. This is discussed in further detail in Victor Pickard, "Toward a
People's Internet: The Fight for Positive Freedoms in an Age of
Corporate Libertarianism," in *Blurring the Lines: Market-Driven
and Democracy-Driven Freedom of Expression,* ed. Maria Edström,
Andrew T. Kenyon, and Eva-Maria Svensson (Gothenburg,
Sweden: Nordicom, 2016), 61–68.

29. Susan Crawford, "First Amendment Common Sense," *Harvard
Law Review* 127 (2014): 2343–91.

30. Timothy B. Lee, "Verizon: Net Neutrality Violates Our Free
Speech Rights," *Ars Technica,* July 3, 2012, https://arstechnica
.com/tech-policy/2012/07/verizon-net-neutrality-violates-our
-free-speech-rights/.

31. Quoted in Susan Crawford, "The Sneaky Fight to Give Cable
Lines Free Speech Rights," *Wired,* December 4, 2018, https://
www.wired.com/story/spectrum-comcast-telecom-fight-win
-free-speech/.

32. Parts of the following draw from Victor Pickard, "Before Net
Neutrality: The Surprising 1940s Battle for Radio Freedom,"
Atlantic, January 29, 2015, https://www.theatlantic.com/tech
nology/archive/2015/01/before-net-neutrality-the-surprising
-1940s-battle-for-radio-freedom/384924/.

33. The concept of conjunctures was famously described by the

Italian theorist Antonio Gramsci. See, for example: Antonio
Gramsci, *The Gramsci Reader: Selected Writings, 1916–1935*, ed.
David Forgacs (New York: New York University Press, 2000).

34. Pickard, *America's Battle for Media Democracy.*

35. For an overview of possible policy interventions against plat-
form monopolies, see Victor Pickard, "Breaking Facebook's
Grip," *Nation*, May 21, 2018, 22–24; earlier digital version
posted April 18, https://www.thenation.com/article/break
-facebooks-power-and-renew-journalism/. See also Shoshana
Zuboff, *The Age of Surveillance Capitalism: The Fight for a
Human Future at the New Frontier of Power* (New York: Public
Affairs, 2019).

36. For an explication of *digital feudalism,* see Sascha Meinrath,
James Losey, and Victor Pickard, "Digital Feudalism: Enclosures
and Erasures from Digital Rights Management to the Digital
Divide," *CommLaw Conspectus: Journal of Communications Law
and Policy* 19 (2011): 423–79.

ACKNOWLEDGMENTS

This book greatly benefited from a group of exceptionally kind and gifted friends and colleagues. We owe a special debt of gratitude to Craig Aaron and Karl Bode, who offered us tremendously helpful feedback on the entire book. Craig, who has been on the front lines of the "net neutrality wars" for many years, offered excellent suggestions, particularly with regards to our analysis of net neutrality activism in chapter 3. Karl Bode is one of the nation's top tech policy journalists, and we were aided by the depth and breadth of his knowledge about net neutrality. Russell Newman, a leading scholar of net neutrality, also gave us encouraging and helpful feedback.

We especially thank Richard John and Dan Schiller, two

of the foremost experts on the history of American telecommunications, for providing invaluable advice on much of the historical context that we discuss in chapter 1. Harold Feld, Christopher Terry, and Matt Wood generously shared their expertise with us on specific law and policy questions. Lauren Bridges, Chloé Nurik, and Pawel Popiel jumped in on several occasions with top-notch research assistance. Three anonymous reviewers provided incisive, challenging feedback that ultimately strengthened the final manuscript.

We are especially grateful to our amazing editor at Yale University Press, Joseph Calamia, who first approached us to write this book. In addition to keeping us on track and providing timely and perspicacious editorial advice, it was Joseph whose original vision made this book possible. We also would like to thank Robin DuBlanc for her masterful copyediting and extraordinary eye for detail, which brought discipline and structure to the manuscript. Any errors, of course, are solely on us.

We also thank our colleagues at the Annenberg School for Communication at the University of Pennsylvania who help create a supportive intellectual community for critical work. We thank our families for their love and understanding, especially in the face of tight deadlines. Victor thanks his brilliant wife Julilly Kohler-Hausmann and her always-supportive family, his heroic mother Kay Pickard, and his loving and lively children Zaden and Lilia (to whom he promised their names would always appear in his books). David thanks his life partner and fiancée Laura Ann Noboa. Her intellectual and spiritual companionship, boundless humor and wit, and enduring love make everything in this life sweeter. David also thanks his parents Edward and Ellen for their patience and unwavering support.

Finally, we would like to thank the many activists and concerned citizens in the United States and around the world who continue to fight for a more democratic communication system. It is their struggle we hope to honor with this book.

INDEX

Italicized page numbers indicate illustrations. Tables are indicated by "t" following the page number.